En Route To Eternity

*For dear Diane,
Together En Route,
Ronda*

En Route To Eternity

The Story of My Life
Ronda De Sola Chervin

The Miriam Press
New York

ISBN 0-939409-02-X

Library of Congress Catalog Card Number 94-79464

© 1994 The Miriam Press, New York

All rights reserved

Manufactured in the United States of America

All inquiries should be addressed to:
The Miriam Press, P.O. Box 798, Highland NY 12528
(914) 691-6496

Contents

Why I Wrote My Life Story 1

The Me Who Was Always a We 3

The Unhealed Family Tree 13

The Girls Who Didn't Fit In 27

In Search of Truth 41

Finding Christ in the Catholic Church 49

Love and Marriage 63

Ties That Bind 73

Defender of the Faith 87

Mid-Life Crisis and Amazing Graces 99

"Out of the Depths I Cry Unto Thee" 115

Epilogue 139

Appendix 143

Why I Wrote My Life Story

To tell the truth, it's scary to write a book about my life. Twenty-page accounts of how an atheist girl from a Jewish background became a Catholic are delightfully easy to produce. In a short amount of space, I can emphasize the positive:

"See, there I was, a sinful wretch, dying of despair at the bottom of the pit, and here comes beautiful Jesus to save me. Amen. Alleluia!"

The motive for writing this book was to try to experience God's love healing not just my spiritual self, but the me of my whole life, from tiny, contingent embryo to fifty-six year old woman. The total me: wife, mother, grandmother, philosophy professor, lecturer, writer, and presently an uneasy mixture of sadness, love, irritability, hope, boredom, fervor, fear and intense yearning for union with God.

I heave my whole life up into the waiting arms of my Saving Christ and beg him to give it back to me redeemed. I hope that this act of faith, and his response, will give me renewed strength to face the next phase of my journey ... en route to eternity.

The Me Who Was Always a We

Unless you are a same-sex twin yourself, you probably have not pondered the effect of never having been without an other body of the same type and age, beginning with close confinement in a warm, dark womb.

My twin sister Carla and I are fraternal twins. Not one fertilized egg that split but two eggs fertilized at about the same time, in New York City in 1936.

About the same time. This seemingly neutral statement has come to haunt me. Fifty years after April 24, 1937, the day of our birth, my father began to talk to us about how he never knew for sure if we were his children at all!

What nonsense! Carla De Sola Eaton, my sister, looks just like him. The same attentive set of the eyes, the same nose and mouth. More from my mother's side, the dark coloring and eyes.

An inner voice said: "Ronda, *you* never looked like anyone in the family." A changeling? Not likely. Twins are enough of an occasion in any hospital, even in crowded New York City, to make mix-ups with a strange baby less than probable.

I asked two doctors about the biology of the embryo. Even though highly improbable, I was told, in the case of fraternal twins, it was just remotely possible that if a woman was impregnated within a very short time by two different men, the eggs could be fathered separately!

Startled, I began introducing the subject into conversation with my mother. In and out of full coherence during her last year of life, it was hard to dig into memories so intimate and far distant. Somewhat annoyed, but not denying the possibility since her life at the time had been experimental and libertine, she surmised that my father was just looking for an excuse for having lapsed in child support when we were teenagers.

Last year, I pressed my father once more. Could he call to mind any time during his long love affair with my mother, before our birth, when, having made love to my mother, she might, on the same day, have been impregnated by another man?

"Hmmmm," my old father paused, intrigued. "Well, yes. There were these folks visiting us once in those days who liked group sex. I was sleepy and didn't feel like getting involved. Who knows?"

After my mother's death, looking through an old photo album, I came upon a man's face. Aha! He looked just like me! The little snapshot was of the type one used to be able to get by sitting in a tiny booth on 42nd street in a penny arcade in New York City. I kept it safely in a folder. From time to time I would peek at it with sly interest. My real father?

Casually, I showed the picture, among others, to Ralph De Sola, the man I had always taken to be my father, asking: "By the way, is this "X"?"...the name of a man I knew my mother had known for ages and taken up with again after my parents' separation.

My father laughed loudly. "Of course not. That's old "Manuel!" Manuel turned out to be a Hispanic great uncle on my father's side.

Uppermost in my consciousness from earliest childhood on was being a twin: describing whatever was happening as *we* are playing, *we* are fighting; from the distance, always called to as a twosome, "Come here, girls."

In spite of the many personality differences all twins have, there is an experience of closeness that no other siblings have to the same degree. Yes, there are reasons for distance. Many. And yet it is impossible for me not to believe that someday we will be living together as little old ladies; to die on the same day; and be buried in the same wooden coffin, huddled together like twins in the womb.

The Me Who Was Always a We

My twin sister, Carla, older by a few minutes and taller and stronger, was the dominant and more creative twin, whom I thought could beat me up if she chose, but also on whom I depended for my fun.

On boring days, I could never think what to do and she was a fund of exciting ideas. At night, frightened of the dark, it was she who could spin out tales about magical eggs sailing along the ceiling, adding an element of awe to my terror. It was I who would take refuge in her bed, never she in mine, for safety from bears who might be hiding in the closet or fires that might come in through the window.

She was more introverted than I; she didn't need me the way I needed her. I recall seething with frustration when occasionally she would exalt in her power over me by getting me to set up the whole monopoly board and then suddenly announcing that she didn't feel like playing after all.

Once in elementary school, P.S. 93 on 93rd Street West between Amsterdam Avenue and Broadway in New York City, I paid her back. In a move I still can only recall with guilt and shame, I wrote her name in crayon on the inner door of a toilet to get her in trouble. Sure enough, she was called in for interrogation. She denied the crime and I don't think she was punished, but was left with the sad feeling of having secret enemies. It was many years before I would "fess up" that I was the one who betrayed her.

Our relationship since childhood has been both close and rocky at the same time, as seems to be the case with many twins. I don't think of my sister and myself as a "we" anymore.

The schism started at the time when she became more and more fascinated with dance and I continued to be a girl of words. I was entranced by her dancing, thinking it the most beautiful thing in the whole world to be able to move with such grace to music. I would watch her modern dance exercises or her own informal or composed dances with glowing delight, constantly praising her for being able to make fresh beauty come alive right in our living room.

But I was too clumsy to do it with her. We were no longer a "we." She became beauty personified, and I was just unformed me. At a time of depression in college, I tried taking up ballet. Although I had plenty of spirit, the discipline was alien to me and I soon dropped out.

Later, when I found my own separate identity as a philosophy professor, I would stop competing to be beautiful and think of myself instead as a seeker and finder of truth. This provided a sort of balance.

Even more, we could not be a "we" as adults for religious reasons. In our twenties, we both converted to the Catholic faith in dramatic ways that will be described later. At first, being Catholics was a great bond. But our paths diverged in the seventies to an ever-widening gulf.

I identified myself totally with the Church. I existed (and still do) to be a Catholic and thought of Church teachings as absolute. Carla defined herself, I believe, more as a deeply religious person, open to many streams of spirituality; part of the Catholic tradition but not constrained by Church laws.

This difference made for heated arguments when we discussed theology. To this day, there is a distance which both of us experience as painful, although the feeling of closeness emerges again whenever I can delight in Carla's beauty as she performs or leads a workshop. It is also there when we pray the rosary together, listen to sacred music, or, most recently, when she could minister to me in an extraordinary way at the time of the death of one of my children.

As a child, the "we" of twinliness was always there. But I was just as bound up in my identity with my mother, for she formed me to be her alter-ego.

Mommy, sometimes called *Momushka* from the Russian, was warmth, laughter, joy, intensity, and above all conversation. She was short, around 5'2", large-breasted, round bellied, affectionate, tender and empathetic.

I always felt Mommy understood me perfectly, loved me boundlessly, and would do anything to shield me from any sort of harm. She always took my part in adjudicating quarrels with my sister.

Cozy evenings were spent reclining on couches reading. My mother would tell us highlights of her book, even narrating whole chapters.

So deeply did reading effect me that I could hardly bear to spend a single day without books. The personalities depicted in fiction seemed to me in some ways more real than living people. Since, in a novel, all kinds of dramatic events spanning fifty years can be read about within five hours, I think fiction increased my notion that life should move along with speed and drama.

I was forever looking for ways to become the characters I loved in books or to identify those around me with them. The most memorable archetypes to me are the *Black Stallion* (image of strength and freedom); Jenny from Robert Nathan's *Portrait of Jenny* (an image of ethereal, graceful, poetic girls and women who remind me of my sister when she dances); Heathcliff of *Wuthering Heights* (the male hero for whom I searched in vain); Scarlett O'Hara of *Gone With the Wind* (an image of wild, passionate, colorful evil); and Tolstoy's *Anna Karenina* (an image of the tragic end of women who make seemingly fated but wrong choices).

Nothing was more wonderful in my life as a child than reading. The trip to the library with my mother was a journey to the next two week's fulfillment. On the way, we would discuss the books we had read during the previous two weeks. On the way back, we could not yet discuss the books carried in our arms, since they were mysteriously hidden within the unopened covers.

Instead we would discuss life in every aspect. So closely did we analyze ourselves, the people we knew, and characters in books, that I truly cannot remember ever having a single thought that was not immediately enunciated and picked apart. If either of us had the misfortune to have to go to the bathroom in the middle of a discussion, the other would stand outside the door and continue talking so that there need be no break in the dialogue! Naturally, such a background was an ideal milieu for the development of a future teacher, writer, and speaker.

A brilliant raconteur, my mother would amuse us with narratives about the people she knew in the past, present friends, writers she encountered in the publishing industry, or events described in the newspaper. I would copy her by trying to describe as colorfully as possible whatever was happening in school or in my books.

How did the "we" of twinliness mesh with the "mother/daughter we"? Not at all. I was either with my mother or with my sister but rarely did we relate intimately as a whole family. My sister was closer to my father than to my mother; and when he left, she grew even closer to me.

I believe now that it was my mother who set things up emotionally so that there was no whole family love, only separate one-on-ones. She had a deep craving to be at one with someone, usually in the capacity of a lover. She was unhappy with my father, whom she never married but lived with in a common-law bond. To her, I became that one perfect friend and even a sort of idol.

I could be close to my twin sister, Carla, only by going off with her to our room, where we would play our own games, or plot mischief: postponing our chores with endless excuses.

To express any love for our father was to risk losing our mother's affection, for they were moving apart way before he left to marry and live with a beautiful younger woman and her teenage daughter.

My father had much love for both of us and spent endless hours sharing with us his interests in music, art, animals, and geography. I always thought, as a child, that he loved Carla more ... they were a "we" from which I was excluded. In later life, however, my sister was to bond with my mother and I was to get much closer to my father.

The leave-taking of my father when we were eight years old served to strengthen and define the bond between myself and my mother. I was somehow to make up for that loss by becoming her ideal companion.

I wasn't jealous of the lovers who started visiting the house, because I could not conceive that she could ever love them as much as she loved me. Even though she was a very sensual woman, attractive to certain bohemian men in her late forties and onward, there was a distrustful, aggressive side to her character that kept her from making permanent relationships with men. Instead she would engage in long, long love affairs.

I had a pre-teen fascination with these men, whom I knew only as conversationalists, not having the foggiest idea what lovers were until I was around fourteen.

There was one friend of whom I was jealous, however. A young ceramist, worked with my mother and adopted her as a surrogate mother. She was a brilliantly witty conversationalist who put me in the shade.

Lily made great efforts to win the friendship of us twins. When she was paying attention to us, we were happy as clams, but the minute she and my mother were engaged with some topic over our heads, we would withdraw into our bedroom to play. Finding out in my teens that my mother was bi-sexual increased the sense that this friend could be a threat.

However, the real menace to my deep closeness with my mother lay not in *my* jealousy of *her* friends. The difficulties began when *I* started dating.

When I was fifteen, I met my first serious boyfriend at the Bronx High School of Science, Aaron Sherman. Having been regaled with stories of my mother's love affairs in Paris, I was hell-bent to enjoy the interesting emotions I associated with falling in love.

Of the men with whom I was to be seriously involved, Aaron was probably the one who had the most of Heathcliff in him. He was tall, dark, intense, individualistic, and rebellious.

To my surprise, my rationalistic mother, who would never tell us to do anything without a long philosophical explanation, suddenly started scolding me for spending hours in a remote room locked in close embrace with Aaron or indulging in similar activities in Central Park. Since she was a libertine hedonist, she could not base her objections on any kind of traditional moral code. I couldn't understand why she objected, and finally forced her back onto aesthetic grounds; somehow what we were doing was vulgar.

But how could the negative of vulgarity possibly compete with passionate love? For the first time in my life, I found that I had to conceal an important part of my life from the mother with whom I had shared every thought and feeling for fifteen years.

The conflict climaxed after a tonsillectomy. Coming out of the ether in great pain, I started begging not for dear old Mommy but for Aaron! If he could be sent for to hold me tight, I would be okay.

You may wonder why it didn't occur to me that my mother was simply worried about an unwanted pregnancy? And why didn't I even think about this? Although I had studied biology and knew the facts of life, I was not contemplating going all the way. Besides, wasn't abortion the way sophisticated anti-religious moderns handled such emergencies? And wasn't my mother an expert at getting rid of babies? So why worry?

In a combination of fear for her beloved daughter and jealousy of this rival, my mother decided that my behavior might be checked by starting psychotherapy, then all the rage. Surely both twins must have been affected by my father's departure from the family hearth? Couldn't such a change lead to some unbalanced need for compensation ... lead us, perhaps, to choose unsuitable boyfriends?

At just this time, it happened that my grandfather gave us a sum of money from the cancellation of a life insurance policy. Off we were sent to Dr. Fink, the psychoanalyst. The results were both humorous and frightening. The most memorable funny outcome was the discovery that we had extremely similar Rorschach tests, seeing the same 50 to 100 items in each picture: identical patterns of neuroses such as workaholism.

The terrifying incident centered around Dr. Fink's theory that all girls and women were afraid of sex. A sign of recovery would be if we would show no fear when he made a surprise sexual advance in the midst of a group therapy session. When I ran away from him in the direction of a fifth floor window, it was supposed to show that I was still immature and in need of further counseling. Alarmed, I suppose, at the possibilities manifested by the race for the window, Dr. Fink desisted in his sexual challenges, though continuing the regular sessions. Soon after that, the money available for treatment ran out.

In spite of my compliance, my mother's motives would cause a rift between us. Why did my mother not approve of my fascinating Aaron? After all, he was a figure out of a novel to me, a lover of literature, a non-stop talker, made even more attractive because he was in the process of rejecting his rather bourgeois Jewish parents. His folks, incidentally, were by no means thrilled with his choice of girlfriend. With a name like De Sola, they were convinced I was a Catholic. The last thing they wanted was an early marriage to a Gentile, due perhaps to a manipulative pregnancy, before their smart son could do them proud at an Ivy League College.

I soon began to think that what made Aaron unsuitable in my mother's eyes was simply that he was someone who might someday take me away from her. It was clear that Aaron did not like my mother. He considered her smotheringly possessive. What young man, intent on taking his girlfriend out for an evening alone, would enjoy spending the first hour in a three-way conversation with her mother?

Nothing would stop me from continuing my first serious relationship. Yet I felt guilty and sad that, given her negative attitude, my mother could no longer be my confidante. Even though I eventually broke up with Aaron, the same basic pattern was to emerge with other men. I desperately wanted to share everything that was happening with my mother, who was my ideal woman and role-model, but I couldn't risk her irrational criticism of my behavior or of the characters of the men I was interested in, even, eventually, my husband. I felt that I always had to choose between the men and women in my life, making one sex more important than the other in any given situation.

In the last years of my mother's life, we felt an urgent pressure to regain a little of the lost love. Paradoxically, this became more possible when she became partially senile.

My husband bridged the rift with tremendous, forgiving, patient love, holding her in his arms when she was frightened and close to death. With no possibility of sustained arguments, my mother and I could hold hands shyly and smile at each other as she lay slowly dying.

En Route To Eternity

And thus, the me who was always a we, with broken ties dangling unfinished behind ... sometimes, I feel like only half a person, condemned to search forever for the other half Writing about my sister in this autobiography has made me more conscious of how vital she was to my sense of identity as a child, and opened up a craving to one day be reconciled ... to become a "we" again this side of eternity.

The Unhealed Family Tree

My mother, Helen Rosenson, was born in Leningrad, Russia in 1899 to Regina and Leon Rosenson. Both my mother's parents died before we could meet them. Due to her unhappiness as a child, she rarely spoke of them or of most of her family. Happily, last year, an investigation into the family tree led to a reunion where I got to meet long-lost now new-found cousins — Ethel, Lenore, Meg, Helen — whose love added to this chapter. It was so interesting to find out how much we were alike in personality!

My mother seemed to have loved her father, a doctor, best, but felt neglected by him due to his busy schedule. Her mother evidently regarded child-raising as a dull burden and left her mostly to the care of the Polish servants who secretly taught their atheist charges how to make the sign of the cross. On the day of her baptism, in a charming gesture, my mother signed herself in the name of the Father, the Son, and the Holy Spirit in Polish.

As you can see from the photograph of Regina Rosenson, she was a beautiful looking person. I often gazed at pictures of her hoping that when I was an old woman I might have some of that tired, melancholy nobility in my face. Now, at fifty-six, when I am not grinning, there *is* a certain resemblance.

Regina Rosenson
Grandmother

Leon Rosenson, from Kharkoff, was a doctor whose family no doubt migrated to Russia, via Finland, during the time when many German Jews were physically imported from Germany because of the Russian belief that Europeans were far ahead of their own backward people in scientific knowledge.

When they lived in Russia the Rosenson family were already atheistic and socialist. Their minds were formed by the Enlightenment mentality associated mainly with figures such as Spinoza. This liberation from religious tradition swept through Jewish society in the nineteenth century, splintering the previously tightly bound Jewish communities into many factions: orthodox believers, reform Jews, Zionists, and total atheists such as my grandparents.

Because of fear of being jailed as socialists, Dr. Leon Rosenson and family left Russia when my mother was one year old in 1900 and eventually settled in Brooklyn, N.Y. My uncle Mitch, slightly older than my mother, still recalled standing by the railroad tracks cheering for the Czar under the title of "The Little Father." Leon Rosenson was an old family doctor, riding in a carriage drawn by a horse through the streets of Brooklyn to visit his patients who were mostly poor, Yiddish speaking Jews.

The Rosensons must have had a haughty superior attitude toward the culture of these Jewish patients, since my mother prided herself on her cultivated accent, abhorring the Jewish intonation in others and despising Yiddish humor and mannerisms. When meeting people, she would often refrain from mentioning that she was Jewish.

My grandfather died in the 1920's. My grandmother returned to Russia after the revolution and died in Leningrad before we were born. What came down to us from the Rosenson family was not a Jewish cultural background but a passionate love for things Russian. I came to love nineteenth century Russian literature the most of any, especially the novels of Dostoevsky and Tolstoy. Slavic ballet music such as the melodies of Tchaikovsky or Prokofiev still send me into wild exaltation.

The Unhealed Family Tree

Helen Rosenson, who would be my mother, went to Hunter College for a short while. She left abruptly, to elope with one Percy Winner, a Columbia student of journalism, leaving a personal "declaration of independence" as a good-bye letter for her parents.

Together the young couple set off for Paris to become part of the famous expatriate cafe society described so well by Hemingway. The marriage did not last.

Helen spent her twenties shuttling between New York and Paris. Her life was studded with love-affairs with both sexes, transitory jobs, and abortions. In young adulthood I picked up the notion from my mother that she had had at least twelve abortions before her pregnancy by my father in her late thirties.

When my father wondered whether they could afford a baby, Helen proclaimed that every woman had a right to have a child and that if he didn't think they were ready (this was during the depression) they would become ready. I marvel now at the thought of how unlikely it was that I would come into the world. If she had not aborted even one of those previous babies, she would never have gone on to us. One child would have been plenty for her. How strange that our lives somehow depended on the killing of so many brothers and sisters! How much God must have wanted exactly us two to come into the world!

Yet every person ever conceived could write the same last sentence. I find it awe-inspiring that each child is utterly unique even from a physical standpoint. You would not have the same face if you had been engendered even a week later!

An utterly undomestic person, my mother had not the slightest idea what to do with the babies she gave birth to at Park West Hospital. My father describes reading in a Department of Health pamphlet for poorer people about how an infant should be inserted into a basket with newspaper underneath its little bottom. They had to call on neighbors to find out what exactly one did with babies to feed them. Happily helpers were so cheap that my parents were quickly able to obtain maid-nannies.

My father's family background was even more unusual. Born in 1908, Ralph De Sola was the offspring of Solomon De Sola, an Hispanic Jewish Atheistic Free-Mason from Curacao, raised in Baranquilla, Colombia who had married a devoutly Christian, Pennsylvania Dutch woman during his years as a dental student at the University of Pennsylvania.

Solomon De Sola's family traced their ancestry back to the Spanish Inquisition. During that ill-fated period, escape from persecution was effected by some Jewish families through conversion, and by others through flight to Holland and subsequently to the Dutch colonies in the West Indies. To this day, there are large families of Jewish De Sola's and others who are part of the Catholic branch. Also, of course, the atheistic ones like my grandfather.

The famous New York City member of the De Sola family was the Sephardic Rabbi David De Sola Poole. Although I had vaguely heard of this rabbi as a child, I didn't meet him until my grandfather's funeral. Amidst the Jewish ceremonials I had been taught to despise all my youth, I was quite surprised by the magnetic, piercing stare of the old Rabbi.

In my forties, reading the famous Marquez novel, *A Thousand Years of Solitude*, I was horrified to realize that it was of the benighted, dirty decadent towns of my ancestors that Marquez wrote with such vivacity and disgust. My father, who often visited Barranquilla as a boy, found it to be fascinatingly exotic.

Another shock came in reading a biography of Oscar Romero and finding on the first page a reference to the De Sola's as among the fifteen most evil families of El Salvador. This judgment my father confirmed from his own knowledge of them.

To return to my grandfather Solomon's Pennsylvania days, it was during his years as an intern dentist that the dashing young Hispanic came upon the mouth and simultaneously the whole beautiful person of pale, blond, sweet Grace Geist, an ardent Christian of a Lutheran and Quaker farming family originally coming to America from Germany. When the infatuated girl told her father that she was thinking of marrying Solomon De Sola from Colombia he naturally wondered what religion his future son-in-law might practice.

"Jewish!" he exclaimed, "there are no Jews now, they all died out in the Old Testament!"

Later, when I became a Catholic, I was quite enchanted to realize that my grandmother's name, Geist, meant Spirit. Grace Geist De Sola was deeply religious, loving the Scriptures above all. Concerning churches, she was experimental, making her way from Quaker and Lutheran to Presbyterian and finally to the Episcopal Church of St. Agnes on 92nd St. and Columbus Avenue in New York. Looking back, I identify her with St. Monica, for she spent many an hour weeping over the antireligious ideas of her husband, the atheism her only son developed as a teenager and never outgrew, and the subsequent atheistic upbringing of her adored twin grandchildren. There is a page in her Bible, marked by her old-fashioned, flowing handwriting: "I pray with tears in my eyes that one day my dear grandchildren will know the love of their Redeemer."

Grace and Solomon De Sola took up their dwelling in the Upper West Side of Manhattan. It was quite an upward move for Grace, from the farm to the sophisticated city. According to my father's unverifiable account, the first baby was born severely deformed and thrown by both parents, whether dead or alive he is not sure, into the basement furnace. I asked my father what he had thought of this extraordinarily violent and horrifying incident. He said that he had always thought it was a smart move. Defective things should be eliminated. I wonder now how his own mild stuttering as child might have been related to fear that if he failed to be perfect he might meet a similar fate. My grandmother's parents upon hearing back in Pennsylvania about the deformed baby told her that this could only be the result of some sort of dirty sex she was practicing. My sister Carla, doesn't believe this story at all. She thinks it was a tale told to get Ralph to be obedient as a child through fear.

For awhile she insisted on abstinence, but then craving a child so much, she relented. Soon after came the birth of my father, a beautiful healthy boy. His earliest memory would be of feeling suffocated under many blankets in his carriage and plotting that one day he would find a way to escape from this imprisonment.

The sex life of my father's parents withered away after his birth. When I was a child visiting them, there was a wooden screen separating their beds. When his son was old enough to understand that the stream of beautiful women being wined and dined in the De Sola apartment were not so much mutual family friends as his father's mistresses, Solomon used his wife's refusal of sex as the reason.

Now my grandfather was a seemingly correct, upright, and quite formal gentleman of the old school. Can it be doubted that my father's hidden gradual understanding of *his* father's hidden sensuality would lead to his life-long hatred of hypocrisy and tendency to enmity with men in authority?

Religious psychologists think that atheism about the existence of God the Father can be rooted in difficulties with one's human father. In my father's vitriolic denunciations of religion, the theme that has survived seventy years of leadership among free thinkers is how a good God could allow evil to exist in the world. The God of religion is seen to be as hypocritical as his father turned out to be.

Plenty of ambivalence. A scene of my childhood carries for me the whole weight of my father's mixed heritage of fear of sex and indulgence in sex. Not unusual in the thirties was the idea that children could be spared prudishness in later life by some degree of nudity in the family home. I don't recall my parents being without clothing most of the time, but they would not hide themselves while dressing and let us run around without clothing a good part of the time.

After our bath we would be allowed to scamper around naked dancing to the music my father played on the phonograph. I recall enjoying this freedom immensely. At the age of around three, suddenly, for no reason I could fathom, my father interrupted a wild dervish I was performing, smacked my behind and yelled "enough is enough." Since neither parent had ever spanked me before or after, this unexpected punishment left in my psyche some kind of permanent sense of caution. Somehow men wanted you to be free, capricious, but only up to a point. You could never know when angry rejection would replace loving delight. Because this shock came when I was naked I think it left an impress of ambivalence in me.

As an adult I tended to combine passionate romantic daydreams about sex with fear about totally letting go.

Now in his eighties, my father speaks of both his parents with great love and respect. One of his reasons for wishing there was a God and an eternity is so that he could apologize to them for all his rebellious misdeeds. As children, however, we were brought up to despise them both: she as a crazy puritanical religious fanatic and he as a two-faced lecher. My sister says we were brought up not to despise them but to ridicule them.

Thinking about this family history now I empathize most with my grandmother. Even if at fault herself for withholding sex from her husband based on prudish attitudes, she must have suffered incredibly from having to be the hostess of these flamboyant lady friends. Even before she realized the true nature of these relationships, there must have been quite a palpable atmosphere of deceit.

My grandfather's prowess in the arena of sex extended way beyond the death of his wife. It does not appear that he felt tempted to marry again, but the black Christian family servant eventually refused to come clean and cook on account of "the cheapies" she said were frequenting the apartment. In his seventies, visiting the brothels of Tijuana, he could still boast of extraordinary potency!

Readers acquainted with the practice of praying over the family tree may want to join me in asking God to redeem this branch of mine with all its sad subsequent history still to be told.

You may wonder at the judgemental and almost flip mood of these heavy disclosures. Actually my reasons for disliking my grandmother and grandfather so much had nothing to do with their marital life. They had to do with being commanded to visit them once a week as children.

My grandmother, a compulsively clean neat woman who swabbed the telephone receiver down with eau de cologne so that no trace of the breath of anyone might taint the next user, thought it her duty to begin each visit by scrubbing our hands and then combing out all the knots hidden underneath my long hair. This was both painful and humiliating, especially because somehow my twin never had knots in her hair!

En Route To Eternity

The good part of the visit came right after this penitential rite. Once cleansed and combed we were allowed to gently play with the beautiful old-fashioned toys that lay in waiting in a cedar chest smelling of moth balls.

There was a sailor boy who belonged originally to my father. It had a key that made it into a music box with the tune of some sea shanty. The best were two nine inch twin dollies with long blond hair, blue eyes, sweet little smiles, lace dresses and pantaloons. They represented my grandmother's idea of perfection and stood in sharp contrast to her twin bohemian grandchildren who mostly wore overalls or brightly colored circle skirts and other contemporary clothing.

When my grandfather died, most of the household possessions were taken by other relatives, but we were allowed to keep the dollies. When I started the draft of this chapter, I had forgotten about the dolls which I had given to one of my grown daughters. In the process of moving she asked if I wanted them back. So, here they are on my writing desk reminding me that there *were* some beautiful memories of my grandmother.

My grandfather never learned really how to talk to children, at least not in his second language. Though he had totally mastered English grammar, his conversation was stilted and formal and therefore utterly boring to us.

Just the same we knew that our grandmother loved us very much, and my grandfather expressed his concern by continuing the tiresome weekly visit even after grandma's death and after my father had left New York. No longer as affluent as before, my grandfather made generous gestures such as giving us the money left over in an insurance policy he was canceling and making an arrangement with a delicatessen to provide us with a free roast chicken every Saturday evening. Since my mother only knew how to cook things that could be quickly made on the top of a stove, this delicious chicken, dripping with gravy after an hour in the oven, was a true luxury.

My father, Ralph, an only child, lived at 64 W. 88th St. in New York City and was baptized in the Presbyterian

Church. Ralphito, as his father called him, had red hair, which he was forced to wear in long curls beyond the usual time for cutting a boy's hair. A thin child, he was overprotected by his mother. Ralph resented this greatly and always dreamed of adventures far from the confines of home.

At the tender age of four, Solomon, his father, instituted a pedagogy it took him many years to understand. While shaving, he would mount his small son on the toilet seat and lecture him on exactly how to avoid contracting venereal disease from prostitutes!

Grace De Sola, unaware of her husband's educational efforts, taught her adored son about more spiritual things such as the love of music, taking him with her to local Church concerts and to the Metropolitan Opera and Carnegie Hall. When his own love of music took the form of a passionate desire to be a timpanist, however, she balked, insisting that drums were not noble instruments. All his life my father regretted that he had not insisted on timpani, for music has always been his first love. In his forties, he joined an amateur opera company and played the drums and other percussion instruments to his heart's content.

Ralph was confirmed in the Episcopal Church, but shortly after, at the age of twelve, wrote the vicar a letter informing him that he could no longer attend services because he had received no valid answers to his many questions about the logic of the Creed. When the letter came to the attention of his mother, she and all the Christian relatives wept, but his Freemason father winked at him.

During voyages back to Colombia with his father, he developed a fascination with the ocean and dreamt that one day he would become a seaman. Between 1924 and 1933, he spent his summers at sea, first as a deck cadet on the Red "D" Line, and later on the Grace Line as a purser. I recently asked him what the most beautiful moment of his life was and he said his first day as a seaman. Still in High School, he shipped out on an exploratory expedition to the Galapagos Islands where he captured iguanas and giant tortoises.

This led to a life-long love of all lower creatures. Unsure about a maritime career due to persistent sea-sickness, his next goal was to become a zoologist. His first book, done for the Federal Writer's

Project, was called *Who's Who in the Zoo*. When we were children, it never occurred to us that our pets were lesser in worth than ourselves. Indeed the photo album is full of portrait shots of our dogs and cats, one favorite showing Emmy, the dachshund, peacefully asleep in my mother's bed. My father used to list Emmy on tax returns as a dependent. He was never caught at this fey trick.

Sent to Swarthmore college, he lived in the same fraternity as James Michener. They grew to hate each other because both voracious readers were competing for the same library books. Too adventuresome to remain in stuffy academe, my father took off for the sea after a year. In spite of having written interesting studies of turtles and such, he was turned down for a job in a Museum of Natural History solely because he was a Jew.

Although my father resembles his Christian mother, and has no traits associated with Yiddish culture since his Jewish father was Spanish, not Polish, Russian, or German, the name De Sola was too famous in New York to camouflage his origins.

Being turned down for a profession he would have loved on such a humiliating basis set up a life pattern of distrust of authority figures. He was a fantastically efficient and intelligent worker at all the many occupations he took up from purser to amateur zoologist, to writer and researcher of some twenty books the most important of which is an *International Abbreviations Dictionary*, microfilm salesman, director of tours to Mexican bullfights from Del Rio, Texas, technical writer for Convair in San Diego, and finally professor of technical writing at a San Diego Community College. Nevertheless, he would always have difficulty with stodgy bosses who resented his innovative genius and also his protests against their own inept directives. Other employees would resent the competence of a man with no degrees who would show them up by his speedy, diligent work patterns.

1935 through 1937 saw Ralph De Sola as a member of the Communist Party. He was drawn into this organization by hatred of the hypocrisy of unfeeling capitalists, and drawn out by disgust with the hypocrisy of a party that could make a pact with its sworn enemy overnight (the Hitler/Stalin pact). He often quotes the dictum then current "If you're not a communist in your twenties you have no heart, but if you're still one in your thirties, you have no head."

Ralph's first marriage was to a leftist woman, Fredrica Abrams, Jewish and bi-sexual. They were married for four years, after which she left him for rather vague reasons, saying she had married him just because she wanted to be married.

By the time he met my mother, also a Communist in 1936, none of that set believed in bourgeois concepts like marriage. She was ten years older than he. They lived together without ever formally marrying. By the time of the birth of myself and my twin sister, they had both not only left the party but agreed to cooperate with FBI investigations of such un-American activities.

In 1945, when we were eight years old, my father fell in love with a Canadian Jewish woman, Dorothy Clair, and moved her and her teenage daughter to New York. This wife was the woman of his dreams: beautiful, warm, vivacious, musical, a gourmet cook, outwardly subservient. She will figure later in turbulent scenes involving our adult attempts at reconciliation with my father. She died of Alzheimer's disease in 1987. My father single-handedly nursed her during her last terrible years. His devotion inspired me to think of the these words of Jesus: *"Love covers a multitude of sins."*

He now lives in a beautiful house in San Diego, filled with delightfully unique folk-art techniques of his own devising — a painting of a ship framed by planks with ship's rope entwined through the holes or pieces of drift wood assembled in the shape of New York City office buildings.

Looking back on this history, I am deeply troubled by my ambivalence toward my paternal grandparents. I bring my memories to You, Jesus and pray:

"You who know all hearts, you see that I know so little about the interior lives of these my grandparents. Would you open my mind and my heart to try to imagine the difficulties of being a man from Marquez' colorful world of Jewish travelers to exotic Colom-

bia without Catholic ideas of purity marrying a woman riddled by fear of sexual sin?

"How delightful he would find the company of Hispanic women friends who understood his language, his sense of humor, his combination of chivalry, romanticism, and sensuality. A man brought up on Cervantes, how could he figure out how to overcome the scruples of a Pennsylvania puritan?

"So much easier to support the wife in style, let her handle homelife, while in secret he indulged the side she would never appreciate.

"Is that how You see him in your mercy, my Jesus? And did the constant prayers of that poor wife win the grace of salvation?

"And what of she? Did You watch this daughter of Yours, baptized, confirmed, faithful to You by her own lights, digging the hole of her own misery deeper and deeper as she tried desperately and so unsuccessfully to control a rebellious son who was bringing her grandchildren up with the same destructive philosophy of life and death?

"When she told her Christian friends to bury her coffin perpendicularly so that when the trumpet of the Last Judgment blew she could be the first to run headlong into Your arms, did you smile? Was her purgatory to swim on her tears into the kingdom?

"Are they reconciled at last to each other in Your mercy?"

❖❖❖❖❖❖❖❖❖❖ ❖ ❖❖❖❖❖❖❖❖❖❖ ❖ ❖❖❖❖❖❖❖❖❖❖ ❖ ❖❖❖❖❖❖❖❖❖❖ ❖ ❖❖❖❖❖❖❖❖❖❖ ❖

Since the writing of this autobiography my father died of a heart attack on June 8, 1993. This seems a proper place to write about this event even though some of what I say here will be even better understood by the reader after reading the whole.

My first response at the news of his death was to go numb and busy myself with practical matters. My father had left clear instructions for the executor of the will — a friend, not one of his daughters, that he didn't want any funeral, but instead wanted to have his brain donated to a local medical school and his body cremated and sent out to sea. My sister Carla wanted very much to pray over the body and so when we arrived in San Diego they postponed the cremation so that we could visit the unembalmed body, neatly laid out in the "slumber parlour" of the mortuary. I had to laugh thinking how my father hated euphemisms to see him esconced in death in a room with pink Victorian couches called the slumber parlour. In fact I could imaginatively hear him laughing with me.

Only his face was visible which looked very serious and noble. The group of visitors to the mortuary included my sister Carla and her husband, myself, and his dear Vietnamese woman friend Tuyet and her son. We all prayed together some formal rosary prayers, some invocations to his guardian angel and saints, and Carla and Arthur went close to his body to pray in their own way.

Although he had told us how the money from the sale of his house would be divided between the three daughters – myself, Carla, and the daughter of his third wife, Dorothy, we were surprised to find ourselves also on a large annuity. It meant a great deal to him to make up for having left us girls that he could give us a large compensation on his death. We felt it to be a healing. I was delighted that my husband, a Depression kid with a great need for financial security, was willing to go along with the sense I had coming out of prayer that I put 1/3 of the legacy into our savings account, give 1/3 to the poorest of the poor, and 1/3 for projects of my choice including a car for one daughter and a color printer for another.

On the spiritual level, the death of my father brought surprising graces. He was an extremely independent man to the point of quixotic, whereas I am very dependent. At his death I felt surges of strength within, as if God had chosen this moment to infuse something of his spirit into my own.

On the other hand, lots of buried anger concerning aspects of childhood came to the surface. It was as if now that this formidable father was no longer on earth to punish me, I could afford to let my disappointments about his character come out more directly as in talking about him with relatives and friends questioning me about my feelings about his death.

Having let out some of the anger I am beginning now — six weeks after his death — to also let in the love he tried to show me during the last fifteen years. I see his eyes brimming over with love for us and his pride in me as writer. Sorting out his belongings and bringing home many of his pictures to fill the walls of my own house, I was joyful and grateful for the sense of bright color and love of life he gave us. I also feel closer to my sister Carla and her husband Arthur. A grace from my father's prayers from the other side?

It happens that when arranging for Masses to be said for my father at the parish church I threw in a few for my mother who died five years ago. My friend, the church receptionist, Dorothy Brooks, put the names together. Suddenly hearing "we pray especially at this Mass for Helen and Ralph De Sola," I was startled. I had not put their names together since I was eight years old. It seemed like a symbol of their mutual forgiveness and reconciliation in Christ, and I thought — if they are together in some way in eternity, then I don't have to hold apart so severely the elements in my own polarized personality such as the crusader part coming from my father and the pleasure-loving part from my mother. I await further healings.

Ralph and Helen DeSola
Ronda's Parents

The Girls Who Didn't Fit In

Up until five years old, my sister and I were happy in our sense of belonging within our own household. In spite of many moves, I remember those years of our life as full of fun. In the course of these years, we relocated from New York City to Island Park, Long Island, and eventually to the country area around Norwalk, Connecticut where my father worked for the first microfilm company, Microstat.

Although most of my life from five on would be spent in cities, I have blissful memories of country from early childhood. Especially, I remember giant trees, low stone boundaries on farms, and a magical pond where we went ice-skating on double blades for kiddies.

The other memory of total comfort is connected with a large black maid who used to hold us to her bosom. Even though my mother was large-breasted and warm, this was something else; comparable to the difference between an electric blanket and a goosedown comforter.

So marvelous was the enfolding warmth of this maid's embrace that it left me with a lifelong attraction to all large, round women. (At the worst time of my life, after the death of one of my children, I was at a Marian conference where one of the speakers was a black woman from Trinidad Tobago called Babsie Bleasdell. I begged her to pray with me. On a hot summer afternoon, she held me close enough to sweat together and smothered me in healing prayer until I could stand the pain. I had selected her for this role just by looking at her picture in the conference program, relying on my deep memory of the black woman of my childhood.)

Every day we would watch the yellow school bus pull up to the corner in front of our house in Connecticut and we would picture what it would be like to get on that bus without mother or father, but of course still a twin "we."

Yet we could feel the excitement in our parents when we arrived instead in New York on the corner of 93 Street and Riverside Drive to live in a large apartment overlooking the Hudson. I still recall the feeling of strangeness yet of adventure standing at Riverside Drive staring at that River and the narrow park where we would play for three years.

Several factors combined to make us feel different, awkward and afraid the first days of school at P.S. 93 on the same street between Broadway and Amsterdam. It was policy in those days to separate twins so they could develop their own individual identity without always competing and being compared. That was quite a shock. We had never been without each other for even an hour of our lives! Then came the injunction that little girls should wear dresses or skirts, not the overalls our somewhat feminist mother insisted were more practical. It was bewildering to think there were authorities who could overrule the judgment of a woman as strong as my mother. Soon, we would notice that all the others mothers wore dresses or suits, often with fur stoles in contrast to our mother's pants and colorful, fitted jackets. I remember that I laughed and laughed when I saw a bumper sticker reading "You're a creep because your mother dresses you funny," or something like that. To this day, I almost never wear pants except for bike riding and I love dresses. This rebellion against my mother's tastes is, I suppose, the reverse of what many girls of the same age did in deciding to wear pants most of their adult lives.

Added to these minor difficulties were the problems that came in the separation of our parents.

Although very attracted to each other when they met, I never think of my mother and father as a "we." There are only rare instances where they showed affection or fondness. Mostly they behaved like associates at a job or allies in dangerous territory. Although they would discuss ideas with vehemence, I don't recall any fights between them. Later, I would learn that at this time, writers about the welfare of children discouraged any public show of difficulty between parents.

The Girls Who Didn't Fit In

My father reports that the family doctor once challenged them in their boast that though on the verge of separation they never engaged in open conflict in front of the twins. "Don't you think they hear the silence?" asked this sage medical man.

Nevertheless, it came as a complete surprise when after a long business trip in Canada when we were eight years old (my father was one of the salesmen for a new invention of the day: microfilm), my father took us on a little walk to the corner of 93 Street and West End Avenue and showed us a picture of a lovely young woman and a teenage girl. He explained that he had met Dorothy Clair and her daughter Lorraine in Canada and that he loved them very much. He had thought that perhaps we could all live together but my mother objected.

As a result, he was going to move to an apartment in the upper eighties near Central Park West and we and our mother would move to an apartment on 93 Street between Columbus Avenue and Central Park. We did not realize it at the time, but the difference in these locations was comparable to say, the difference between the red properties in Monopoly and the light blue ones. Riverside Drive where we lived as a complete family was mostly a place for upper-middle class people and the block between Columbus and Central Park was lived in mostly by working class and lower-middle class people. The rent for a four room apartment with kitchen and bath was fifty dollars.

In response to my father's announcement, neither my sister nor I said a word. Our father concluded what must have been for him a painful encounter with the promise that he would be seeing us once a week on Sundays and that he would help financially. Some of my best memories are of my father with consummate patience helping us learn how to ride two-wheel bikes in Central Park, a skill that brought me much pleasure through the years, and later sitting through sentimental musicals he hated because he knew it would give us so much pleasure. I recall him sitting through hours of Fred Astaire and June Allyson type movies, dryly remarking from time to time "Now, they're sure to start singing."

A few months after my father left, my mother started working, first part-time, as a secretary at the Child Study Association, then as an assistant to George Lawton in writing a book entitled *How to Be Happy Though Young*, and finally full-time as an editor at Vantage Press. She loved these jobs and would tell us marvelous stories every evening over dinner about everything that happened at work.

It must be remembered that in those days, hardly anyone divorced. Not knowing that they had never been married in the first place, we were told it was a divorce, possibly to obviate the off-chance that we might someday think of ourselves as fitting the onerous label of "bastards."

In fact, even after finding out that my parents had never married, the idea that we were bastards never crossed my mind until twenty-five years later when Dorothy, who did insist my father marry her, was in an early phase of Alzheimer's and didn't quite know what she was saying. Coming off the train from San Diego to visit our home consisting then of myself, my husband, two twin daughters, and son, she laughed loudly, pointed at me and greeted me with these words: "Oh, it's one of the little bastards!"

At the announcement of my father's leave-taking, because I felt myself to be much closer to my mother than to my father, I truly did not consciously feel any sadness about this separation. I often wonder whether, without the help of a great deal of reading and discussion about psychology, I would have myself made any connection between the separation from my father at a relatively early age and my tendency to form extremely dependent bonds with fatherly men.

However, I made a rather unexpected decision at the time, the significance of which I would only ponder later in life. Up until the separation, I was called Diana, at home and in school, for that was my given name. However, right after my father left, I insisted on adopting a new name: Ronda. This was the name my father always told me he had wanted for me.

Jokingly my father had told me that the day we were born he happened to be standing on a dock overlooking the Hudson River. He was searching for two names that could go together for the twin girls whose femaleness had just been revealed. He noticed a steamer with this designation: Royal Oriental Nuts and Dates Association.

The Girls Who Didn't Fit In

Reading the capitals in sequence the name came out Ronda which corresponded to the Ronda Valley in the famous El Greco painting *The View from Toledo*, a work of art that had always delighted him. Toledo, Spain was the home of our remote Sephardic Jewish ancestors. I believed this whimsical story for decades, only learning recently that whereas the El Greco part was true, the rest was sheer fancy.

In any case, I informed family and school officials that I hated the name Diana because my sister teased me by calling me Danny, a boy's name. My name change was accepted, leading to my sister immediately calling me Ronnie, another boy's name just to get my goat, and as a still further fond diminutive, Roonoo the Rat. The latter appellation was combined in fierce battles between us with the shrieked out childhood exclamation: "I pity your husband." Although I certainly was no passive victim of my sister's anger, most often myself fomenting fights, I don't recall ever insulting her for the simple reason that I looked up to her with adoring love.

Although I always felt that she was wrong about the details of any dispute, I also "knew" beyond a shadow of a doubt that I was an evil little girl about whom no insult could be false. Writing this now, I am startled to realize that no matter how much healing I have received in the area of self image, nothing has yet dissuaded me of the idea that I am an evil little person, now after middle-age spread, an evil short fat person whom everyone would despise if only they knew me through and through. Sigh!

⁂

The move to 43 W. 93 at the time of the separation led to more feelings of not fitting in. To describe the neighborhood first: on one side of the block between Columbus and Amsterdam there were brownstones inhabited by working class Irish Catholic families with rough kids who played handball on the opposite corner against the wall of the Brown Derby Bar and Grill. This bar was the only part of our side of the street that was still Catholic turf. The rest, until the Puerto Ricans moved in, was lower middle class Jewish, culminating on the corner of Central Park West in a Prep School for Boys. Central Park West itself was a completely different territory, filled with large handsome apartment buildings of about fifteen stories inhabited by upper-middle class Jews and some Protestants.

Our apartment building was a step higher in rent than the brownstones, but lower in value than any of the others on our side of the street. For example, although the lobby had a marble floor, there was a filthy, hand-pulled dumbwaiter for garbage collection and seasonal cockroaches to be exterminated sometimes by the superintendent but often by us. Cockroaches were the absolute symbol of poverty in New York City.

The inhabitants of the house were mostly leftist, atheist Jews although there was one orthodox family with many babies. Since my mother was an atheist anti-Communist previously "married" to an informer, it was impossible for her to make friends with anyone in the building. Polite but distant with the neighbors, she would invite her own bohemian friends to visit or go off herself usually to Greenwich Village cafes.

The neighborhood, later to become the site of West Side Story when the Puerto Ricans came, was populated during our childhood by ninety percent Jews and ten percent Catholics. I think the few Protestants went to private schools. We never met a single one.

Almost all the Catholics went to parochial schools. Most of them looked like juvenile delinquents. They branded in my consciousness some bizarre association of wearing a crucifix with being tough and sexy.

We greatly feared these Irish Catholics, even the small ones. I recall a little bully called Johnnie who "owned" the block of 93rd between Columbus and Central Park. He would block the road with his tricycle, daring anyone to walk past. His large, unkempt mother would hang out of the second story window of their brownstone apartment watching the scene.

We were afraid to come home from school, because Johnnie might beat us up. Annoyed by our complaints, my mother decided to leave work early, meet us at school and walk down the block with us. Sure enough, there was Johnnie, grinning mischievously and uttering his threats. My mother, always for reason, explained to him that the block belonged to all of us and he should get out of the way. When he showed no sign of interest in her opinions, she noticed the mother in the window.

"Are you Johnnie's mother?"

"Yeah!"

"Well, Johnnie is frightening my daughters. Please tell him to leave room for them to walk."

"Oh yeah! Whaddid they do ta him?"

My mother turned on her heel and suggested that we go a block out of our way to skirt the dangerous turf. I recall feeling amazed. Could there be stupid, vulgar people who had power over brilliant, intellectual adults? It seemed so. The knowledge of this greatly increased our fear and caution.

Another encounter with Catholics came once when Carla and I were walking home and were suddenly surrounded by a group of preteen Irish delinquents.

"What's your religion?"

We froze and gave no answer.

"I bet you're Jewish. We're gonna beat you up."

"Oh, no. We're not Jewish."

(In those days we didn't realize we were of Jewish ancestry since we were taught to call ourselves Americans or atheists in answer to prying questions of those fools who still thought such matters counted. We were finally told of our Semitic origins when we wondered why we couldn't take off either Catholic or Jewish holidays.)

"Well, what are you then?"

"We're atheists,"

we answered, accurately. Nonplused by this unknown word, the toughs let us go.

It was only in my fifties that I realized that my strong attraction to certain kinds of tough Irish men dates to that period. If you could get the bully to love you then no-one else would dare to beat you up.

The Jews in the area were mostly reform Jews, second generation from the families in *Fiddler on the Roof* who settled on the lower east side but whose grown children migrated to the upper west side when they became successful. They would go to religious services on high holy days. We didn't fit in with them because we were atheists and lower-middle class professionals rather than upper-middle class business people. My parents derisively called the majority of their neighbors the "gilded ghetto Jews."

There was a sprinkling of orthodox Jewish families whose men and boys dressed in black with earlocks and ritual garments. These we thought of as utterly superstitious survivors of the olden times. We never spoke to them.

Then there were the leftists, atheist Jews, and one or two Zionist Jewish families who dreamed of moving to Israel. We didn't fit in with them because we were fiercely anti-Communist and also anti-nationalist.

A new friend, a Catholic psychotherapist, Ross Porter, who is reading this book as I write it, raised a question about how often I seemed ready to be amused about incidents such as being scolded the first day of school for our overalls that others would admit to be wounding. The question intrigued me.

I think I adopted such an attitude very early on. Anything that happened to us was to be food for anecdotal recital — not for tears. This extended even to shedding nary a tear when my father told us he was leaving us to set up another family. Yet I would cry bloody murder if I had to have a splinter taken out!

By fourth grade, another cause of feeling different entered our lives. It was the era in education where bright children were routinely skipped ahead regardless of physical or psychological maturity. Intelligent little girls that we were, with a colossal background in reading, we skipped third grade, half of fifth, and eventually eighth grade in Junior High. This led to surprising hiatuses ... imagine a Ph.D. who never studied the rudiments of grammar and whose education simply left out all classical literature! I am not sure when "its" can go without an apostrophe or which gods were Greek and which Roman and what adventures they had (a lack which renders most English poetry unintelligible). I don't know what an adverb is and the only great literary works I know of the time before the eighteenth century are the plays of Shakespeare!

The academic consequences of being skipped only registered later in life, but the emotional ones were much more immediately painful, although I never attributed the difficulties to the real cause, which was simply being much younger than our classmates.

First of all, I was always the shortest. My twin was in other classes and was a good two inches taller in those days. On the positive side, this meant that occasionally taller girls would pass me on their way to the back of the line and squeeze me fondly with the words "Oh, you're so little and cute!" On the negative side, this helped me develop some of the disordered syndromes called the "eternal child." I learned that in order to curry favor with larger, older, people it was necessary to be childish, funny, and dependent. At fifty-six, I still have the nervous giggle of a little girl.

Whereas we would have been A+ students at our own age level, we were generally about B+, and in the highly competitive schools we attended, B+ was looked down upon greatly by the truly brainy, 160 IQ kids we envied.

The shame of this has had a happy result. As a teacher and speaker I refuse to cater to the top minds in the audience. Never wanting anyone to feel intellectually inferior, as I did, I always popularize ideas in such a way that everyone can understand. This has won me much love from the confused in classrooms and lecture halls. At one workshop, a woman proclaimed that by my easy, amiable style of presentation, I had healed her of her fear of New York Jews!

By seventh grade, when some girls were already thirteen years old to our eleven and a half years, we suffered greatly from being physically less developed than the "sexy" ones. We felt like creepy kids instead of budding females. I will never forget the miserable feeling of walking unnaturally slowly a half block behind the popular girls to avoid the unpleasantness of having them purposely snub us by hurrying ahead not to be seen next to us.

These feelings of inferiority were compounded by the gulf between the family incomes of most of the girls and ours, as evidenced most of all in clothing, but also in allowances. By Junior High, some of the richer girls wore a different cashmere sweater every day, with skirts and even socks ironed by the maid. We were given ten dollars on August 30 each year to buy two new sweaters and one skirt, another five dollars going for one pair of shoes. The rest came secondhand from the thrift shop.

We would go home for lunch to eat a peanut butter and jelly sandwich. The rich girls would buy huge, luscious roast beef sandwiches for fifty cents at the Jewish deli. I wonder now whether the habit we adopted of throwing our sandwiches down the dirty old dumbwaiter was just because we didn't like peanut butter and jelly or more symbolic of rejecting this symbol of relative poverty: a tiny exemplification of the spirit with which, sometimes, people from minority ghettos burn down their own neighborhoods during riots!

Many parents made their girls ask us embarrassing questions about our lack of religion and the "divorced" status of our mother. When they learned that no one was home in the afternoon and that we were allowed to jump up and down on the furniture and whatever else we wanted they began to forbid their children to visit us.

I remember the awful feeling of the first birthday party (at nine) when we were allowed to invite school friends. We gave out about seven invitations and went out to buy party favors, much cheaper than those we would receive at the parties of the gilded ghetto girls of West End Ave. None of the girls came. I remember fingering endlessly a yellow piece of soap in the form of a lemon which was to be the prize for some contest and hating to go to school the next day to face the girls who pretended they had forgotten to come.

A solution I found to the problem of not qualifying for the superior "in" group turned out to serve me all the rest of my life: find the interesting mavericks and in "reverse snobbery" pretend you don't like the popular people. By ninth grade in Junior High I had helped form a little group of girls who met once a week in each other's houses to enjoy refreshments and then go to play in the park. Our baseball games in the park I found blissfully fun and exciting even though I was clumsy and always the worst. I loved the camaraderie and the vast expanses of beautiful trees and rocks that contrasted so much with the dirty surrounding streets.

Refreshment time was more problematic. I would save my allowance for six weeks in order to have enough to buy the requisite cokes and chocolate graham crackers as against my mother's frugal suggestion that I serve frozen lemonade and a cheaper varieties of cookies.

I will always remember the first time it was my turn to serve. Having been able to afford only three bottles of coke for six little girls, I opened the three of them at lunch and divvied them up among six small juice glasses. When the girls arrived after school one of them started laughing. "Ronda, silly, you let out all the fizz by pouring them out so many hours before we came."

I felt utterly mortified. After that, whole bottles of coke and chocolate graham crackers became my favorite after school foods to be indulged in many years after our group dispersed.

My adoration of other foods had a similar origin. Too poor to buy more than one half pound of bacon a week, we would have one slice a morning with one egg; never two slices or two eggs. I still feel like a millionaire whenever I order a side of bacon or two eggs instead of one.

You would think from all of the above that our youth was pretty miserable. In an effort to come to grips with the sufferings of my childhood I have emphasized the negative so far. But there was plenty of joy.

Consistently, unlike so many other children, I loved school. I liked the orderliness of that world of distinct periods of time marked by ringing bells, parallel lines of children, teachers who seemed so certain about what they taught, lined notebooks. All this was a kind of relief from the wild exuberance of our arty home with parents so colorful but so lacking in tranquillity.

Especially, having been a Momma's girl, I found it easy to love my women teachers and lapped up their approval, always doing my work punctually and quickly. It always seemed possible to ingratiate myself with them by showing that I loved and appreciated them. This made up for always being among the mischievous group, running down the corridors during bathroom breaks, laughing during class and falling in with minor dishonesties such as hiding the property of others. Because they knew I loved them, the teachers would always blame someone else for anything wrong.

The other source of youthful joy was the appearance on our scene of an older girl who would be our best friend between the ages of eight and fifteen. Carole Rosenbaum, of a Jewish atheist family, somewhat leftist but not to the degree of others in the house, lived on the same floor in our new apartment near Central Park. A year and a half older and much more sophisticated, she took us over mainly because she was so lonely. Her older father was deathly ill and spent all his time in a room away from her glamorous mother. Her older brother was away at a boarding school. Her mother spent almost all day and late into the evening outside the home, not working but always mysteriously busy.

Left on her own after school from 3 to 10 P.M., Carole craved company. In those days young girls didn't spend too much time out on the town or visiting friends more than a few blocks away and so, even though Carole was popular, richer, a girl of the in-group, she still had afternoons and evenings with nothing to do but play with we twins.

We couldn't be happier. The minute we got home we would rush to her apartment, come home for a quick dinner, race through our homework, and then between 7 and 9:30 go to Carole's house to play cards, listen to 78 rpm musical comedy records, and watch TV — mainly *I Love Lucy*. Brought up to think only low-brows played cards or listened to popular music, we were enthralled with these forbidden activities.

Carole seemed to be endlessly merry and resourceful. Besides playing games and records, she could initiate us in still more dangerous games such as throwing water bombs off the sticky tar roof, or petty theft from candy stores. One year, I arranged to meet Carole for a visit to the old apartment house. We ran up and down the stairs, and walked on the roof. In spite of being on different sides of the fence on many issues, we felt such love for each other, such joy in sharing.

As high school girls, it was Carole who introduced us to her own marvelous circle, made up of the offspring of other atheistic humanists who did square and folk dancing at the Ethical Culture Society youth groups and the Unitarian Church. For the first two years, being among the youngest, my sister and I had to endure the status of wall flowers and occasional partners. By the time we were sixteen, my sister having become a serious student of modern dance, was an expert folk dancer, and I had become less gauche and more acceptable as a partner too.

Then came my father's public case against Anna Rosenberg, whom he felt was a Communist (not Julius and Ethel Rosenberg who went to the electric chair). The bad publicity about this case made it necessary for my father to leave New York where he couldn't get a job — not because he was an anti-Communist informer, but because having been an ex-Communist, he was not trusted! Since my mother had failed to back him up, he became convinced that she was a secret Communist herself.

Having decided to pull up stakes and head west with his wife, my father arranged for our last Sunday together. As usual, we met at a movie house. We were then about fourteen and sophomores at the Bronx High School of Science. My father paid for the tickets to the movie, but this time there were only two tickets. Abruptly and publicly, perhaps because he was afraid of tears, he announced: "I am leaving New York. Your mother is a secret Communist. Go into the theater and watch the movie. Decide whether you want to stay with your mother or go off with me. If you decide to come with me, just walk over to my house after the movie."

We sat through the movie, left in silence and walked back, without any discussion, to our mother on 43 W. 93 Street. For me, there could be no choice. My mother loved me passionately. I loved my father but had never felt close to him, and I felt terribly awkward with his new wife. I do not know why my sister, who had always felt misunderstood by my mother and close to my father, seemed to have not the slightest doubt. Maybe she felt uncomfortable with Dorothy. We would not see our father again for seven years, hearing about him only through our grandfather. Unemployed at that time, he ceased the child-support he had kept up between our eighth and fourteenth years.

To sum up the memories of this chapter, my sister and I were different from the other girls around us in many ways: Spanish/Russian/German in ancestry vs. Polish; atheist vs. nominally Jewish; poor vs. affluent; from a divorced home vs. an intact one; younger vs. more mature; right-wing vs. leftist.

Being different must be something I am used to. Here I am at age fifty-six, a zippy New Yorker in laid-back Los Angeles; one of a very few women teaching in a male seminary; and the only Catholic at my work from a Jewish background. No wonder I always feel so insecure on a psychological level.

The joy is that the only way to feel secure is to be so close to God that He is my all. And, after all, that is what we are all invited to do. The impetus, I have found, is rarely idealistic. It comes from terror in its many forms.

In Search of Truth

Academically, my years in High School were somewhat uneventful. Although I had loved math and science in Junior High, the Bronx High School of Science classes in these subjects seemed to leap ahead into regions beyond my gasp. Pretty soon, I was memorizing rather than understanding, in the process losing all zest for these previously favorite subjects.

What I loved best was composition, literature, and current events. I hung around the fringes of the English department crowd, a maverick minority at a school devoted to Science.

I can remember one significant moment in my High School career. A composition teacher requested we do a one-page paper during class time on the topic "What I Want to Be as an Adult?" To her surprise and mine, I came up with this question: "How can I decide what to do in my life, if I don't know the meaning of life?" Having gotten a rare A plus for this effort, the question lingered in my mind and became a prophesy for my engagement in philosophy and later in faith.

※※※※※※※※※※※※※※※※※※※※※※※※※※※※※※

There were lots of nasty, frightening moments that took place on the long subway ride each day. In those days, and probably still today, there were certain men who got their sexual kicks from choosing less frequented sections of the cars and exposing themselves to young girls either in the form of what we now call flashing or going further to ejaculating while we watched, transfixed as rabbits hypnotized by pythons.

After a few such scary encounters, we learned to run away as soon as something began to happen. These encounters led to permanent suspicion of any man on the subway whose hands were not obviously occupied with something else such as holding onto the strap or rail. Finally, my mother reported the matter to the police. For awhile they sent plainclothes agents with us into the trains after school. We were given a simple signal to display if any of these men started anything. Nothing ever happened when we had an escort. I recall once running with my sister to the front car to tell a conductor about one of these flashers as we had been instructed to do by the police. To our disillusionment, this uniformed official replied "You want me to do it too?" Chilled, we exited at the next stop even though it wasn't ours, the sense of being without protection greatly augmented. I was surprised and interested to learn that nowadays such incidents are included in lists of sexual abuse.

Although ninety percent of Bronx Science students go to college, I was not too sure about it. Both my mother and father had dropped out of college after a year preferring the adventures of Paris or of the sea. I had never heard anything as exciting about life at the University.

In my Junior Year of High School I had taken a quicky shorthand course and worked at temporary summer jobs. That was enough to persuade me that I didn't really want to go into the business world as a secretary. My sister, Carla, was heavily into modern dance. So she had a compelling alternative to college, but since her dance classes took place in late afternoon and evening, she thought she would have plenty of time for college during the day. We finally decided to follow the lead of many of our fellow students and enroll at City College Manhattan. This was in 1953.

In those days, one didn't have to declare a major. We just signed up for an array of mostly liberal arts courses and waited to see where they would lead. After a half year there was a pattern. In every course, I found myself bored by the basic subject matter. Whether it was psychology, political science, or business, I wanted to find out the truth with a capital "T" and the professors were only interested in surveying pluralistic ideas within their field.

I wanted to know not how many theories psychologists could come up with about human behavior, but which one was really accurate. I wanted to know not how many forms of government had existed in the world, but which one was the best. I wanted to know not how many methods there were for marketing products but whether there was a right and wrong about it.

Happily, as a second semester freshman my eyes lit upon a subject I had never even heard of: philosophy. It took me only one day to realize I had finally found the place where I belonged. Philosophy deals not with particular areas of knowledge but with fundamental questions such as the meaning of life itself: what is truth? what is real goodness? Here was the one subject that started with concepts and never left them. What was more, here was a field where a mind honed razor sharp by home debate could be used to advantage.

The first readings we did were from the *Dialogues of Plato*. I loved the figure of Socrates, a man who devoted his whole life to conversing, undermining superficial clichés, thinking with able wit. My entire childhood had been an unending dialogue and here it was again, to the nth degree.

Unfortunately, in that era the whole emphasis in American philosophy was not to glean truths from the masters of the past, but rather to use their writings as matter for critique. We were trained to demolish anything that pretended to the status of truth. Skepticism reigned triumphant.

After my sophomore year, I decided to switch to an out-of-town college. At the time, my motive was to use the combination of my State Scholarship and money saved from summer jobs (in those days, all that was needed was $1,500 a year for tuition, room, and board) to seek the merry, fun life I had read about in novels about college girls.

Underlying this rather frivolous reason was something more primordial. City College was not a good place for me in terms of the search for true love. In two years I had found no boyfriends at all, not to mention any that could compare to Aaron and his friends who had all gone to faraway Universities.

I loved my first year at the University of Rochester, the place I had chosen to go for my out-of-town spree. I was part of an honor's program of some fifteen students who all knew each other pretty well. Instead of going to regular lecture classes, we read articles and books in the library, wrote long papers with ten carbon copies (this was before Xerox) and attended three hour seminars where these papers would be discussed on a professional level.

To add to my happiness, I was quickly accepted into the "in-out-group," that is, the small population of New York Jewish girls, agnostic or atheistic, who lived on one wing in the dormitory and spent their social time with boys who were, if not Jewish, at least very arty. I immediately formed close friendships with young women who seemed much like myself–excitable, unstable, yearning, confused, and on the verge of despair.

To my surprise, the majority of the students at the University of Rochester were believing Christians of various Protestant denominations. I had never met any real believers, and I spent little time with them for they always seemed to be discussing theological topics as abstruse to me as listening to people discussing the differences between dwarfs and elves, just as if they really existed!

All of the young women of my set were on the verge of first love affairs. Once entered upon we became saleswomen for the excitement of it, trying to convince any Christian students we might meet that they should throw off the shackles of superstitious morality and have some fun.

I will not enter into detail about the love affairs that followed because mentors have warned me that reading such accounts can lead others astray no matter how well the tragic outcome is described. Suffice it to say, I and my close friends entered into a pattern of falling madly in love with someone or someone falling madly in love with us, feeling ecstatic at the start, then entering into premature intimacy with fear of pregnancy, and then breaking up when we had squeezed the orange dry.

Each slightly delayed menstrual period would bring daydreams of rushing off to Mexico for an abortion should it be necessary (thank God I never had this need since I believe I would surely have gone ahead and destroyed any baby that was conceived during this time, in a thoughtless imitation of my mother... abortion was only an unpleasant piece of the scenario of fascinating liaisons). I failed to get pregnant partly by luck and then by the stratagem of going to

Planned Parenthood, pretending to be married, and getting a diaphragm.

The man I loved who had the greatest effect on me was a German Fullbright student, Gustav Kemperdick. Working on a graduate degree in American Philosophy for the University of Munich, this man had some of the romantic aura I associated with my mother's tales of Parisian men. Actually he was much more like a character out of the novels of Hermann Hesse. He was about ten years older than I and wore either an expression of amused cynicism or one of beautiful, tragic despair, both equally appealing.

Our time together would be spent lounging on dirty cushions on the floor of his cheap apartment, smoking Gaulois cigarettes, eating cheese and crackers, sipping liquors, and listening to Lotte Lenya discs. He hoped that I would seek a grant to study philosophy Germany and that someday we would marry. Unfortunately, as well as being fascinating, he was a real brute. He had learned violent ways as a youth during World War II and though passionately pro-Jewish enjoyed sadistic verbal teasing and occasional physical violence. When bored, he knew exactly how to work me up into a lather of rage.

Since I had not the faintest idea that genuine love might have anything to do with goodness or kindness, his behavior never struck me as indicating hate or even ambivalence. I just knew that even though I was in love with him he made me miserable and so I hesitated about leaving for Germany a year afterwards when I was offered the necessary Fullbright. By the time I was ready to make up my mind about Gustav, I was already in the ambiance of the Catholic philosopher, Dietrich Von Hildebrand. In answer to my questions whether one was obliged on romantic grounds to marry someone one felt so bound to regardless of how unhappy he made one, he replied sagely that "marriage is not a penance."

To return to my senior year at the University of Rochester, skepticism coming from the study of philosophy with professors who would never show a commitment to any truth even if they personally believed in it, was joined by cynicism coming from my miserable love life.

There were tiny, inexplicable openings to religious meaning, but nothing strong enough to engage my whole mind, heart and soul until my twentieth year. These incidents will be described as part of the spiritual drama of the following chapter.

In spite of being unsure if philosophical studies would ever yield any truth I could live by, I was unsure what else to do after college. I had a literary notion that if I lived alone while seeking an M.A. and Ph.D., reading at my own pace from the great masters while taking required courses to retain my fellowship, somehow I would finally find the truth.

Having a Woodrow Wilson Grant for graduate work, I could choose any University for my studies. At the suggestions of my college department chair, Lewis W. Beck (the Kant scholar), I decided on the rather small department of Johns Hopkins in Maryland. My mother came down to Baltimore with me to help me locate an apartment, some skimpy but colorful thrift shop furniture, a mattress to sleep on, and a cat for company.

It seems that everything at this prestigious university was calculated to bring me to despair. The professors were all scholars more interested in the history of philosophy than the search for absolute truth. The students were busy competing for scholarships by figuring out how many names of obscure philosophers and commentators they could mention per class hour. Years later I would find out that some of these men did pursue truth for its own sake once out of the graduate school game.

The most attractive male students were married. The University was huge. For security, the one other woman student, a Jewish refugee from the concentration camps, and I huddled with our own confreres. My loneliness for a male friend led to panic.

Living alone off campus was not only isolated and sad but also failed to bring the Truth. Although I read religious authors such as Kierkegaard and Dostoevsky at home to balance the skepticism of the philosophers I was studying in the classroom, I imbibed from them only a conviction of the pervasiveness of evil and self-deceit. The hope they preached was barred to me for I had no key to reaching the Christ they loved and trusted so profoundly.

Finally one dark night of my first Fall semester at Hopkins, having found neither truth nor love, I began to fantasize about suicide. I was sufficiently frightened to call up a fellow student and beg to stay the night. The next day I moved in with my Jewish woman friend, begging to share her small dorm room rather than risk coping with my despair.

Still shaky, I left for a Thanksgiving vacation at home. And this was when God began to claim me for His own in ways even I could respond to.

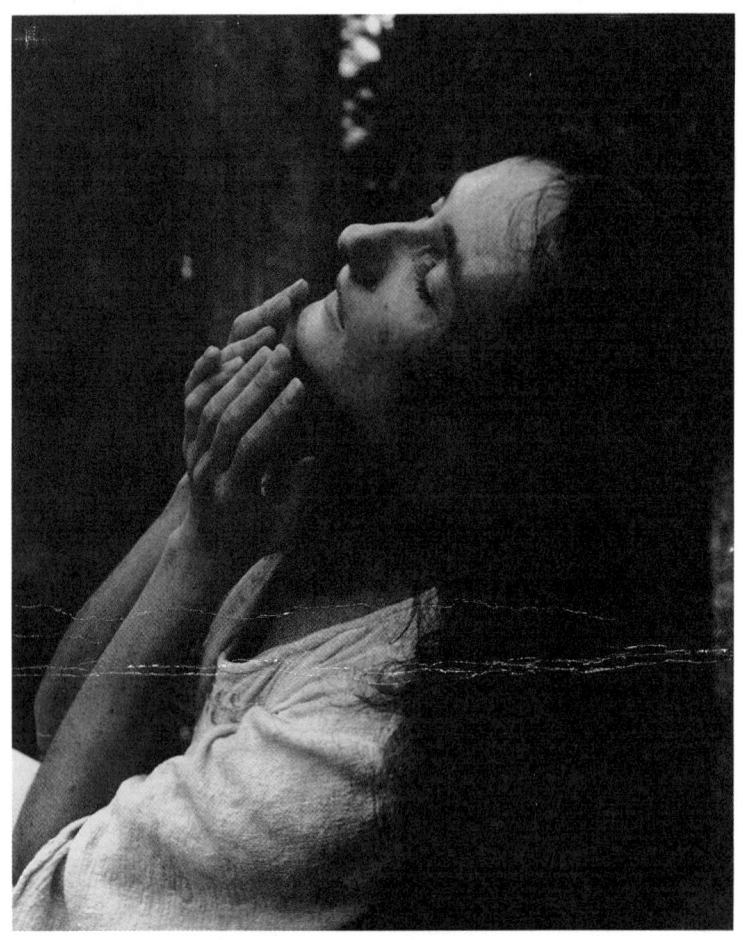

Carla De Sola —Sacred Dancer

Finding Christ in the Catholic Church

Writing about my childhood and youth fills me with awe. What opening in all of this for Christ? In spite of the gigantic wall created by such thorough-going atheism, there were a few little cracks even before my twenties.

My father tells me that when we were little girls around seven years old, we once asked "what is that strange building?" Told that it was just a Catholic Church, we asked what was inside. It was a Sunday. Even so my father decided to bring us in, sure we would be bored very quickly. I have no memory of this occasion, but he reports that we sat through two Masses, fascinated by the goings on.

I believe there were but two Catholic teachers at the public schools I attended. One fourth grade teacher chose to invite the one Catholic boy in class who happened to be part of his Church choir to come in his long gown and sing Adeste Fidelis. I was stunned at the beauty of his voice. Another teacher of music mounted a production of a native American motif play for children. I was in the chorus. She mentioned that she was surprised at the passionate way I sang of the "Great Spirit, Fire on High." Later I would wonder if she had prayed for this totally unbelieving girl who seemed so rapt in this evocation of the divine.

What I also remember with tenderness is the beautiful Christian singing that was part of the interdenominational service at YMCA camps we attended. The Jewish kids were not obliged to go, but again, I suppose, we went out of curiosity. Something piercingly sweet emanated from those hymns and from the faces of our otherwise sporty camp counselors as they led the songs.

As a teenager, I read the famous *Autobiography of a Yogi* and felt envy at the idea of anyone finding a guru who could lead them into some other level of consciousness.

I now believe that it was the Holy Spirit who wanted to give me a glimpse of the holy in such ways. How else to explain the stronger experiences that followed? Just before the trip to the University of Rochester for my last two years of college, I happened to pass an old shop with dusty looking antiques and pictures in the window. Something drew me to a cheap print of Dali's Crucifix — the famous one with the cross suspended in the air. Although I did not particularly like art, I bought this picture of Jesus and hung it on the wall in my dorm room. Since most of the young women in my wing were Jewish, naturally they asked me why a Jewish atheist would have a print of Jesus on her wall. I said I didn't know, I just liked the painting.

My next mysterious religious experience came when a boyfriend introduced me to the music of Bach. A far cry from Ravel's Bolero, I was sure I would find a choral work, Wachet Auf, by an old composer, very dull. To my shock, after ten minutes, tears started rolling down my cheeks. Soon after, I selected Bach's Magnificat from the shelves of Sam Goody's. Trying it out on the phonograph at the store, I went into an ecstatic state of joy. I brought it home and danced wildly to this proclamation of the Virgin Mary. In both cases, I paid no attention to the words, but simply felt something sublime in the music.

The German philosophy student I had been so in love with happened to have a deep reverence for the Catholic Church, even though he himself was an agnostic. During World War II, there was a German Catholic priest who got close to some of the lost youth of that terrible time, Gustav being one of them. Most of his Protestant friends became Catholics as a result of this priest's love for them and his heartfelt manner of conveying the truths of the Church.

Gustav didn't make the leap, but he planned to do so some day in the future. His ironic way of expressing this desire was to say "Someday, when I am lost in the darkness of a pit, I will need something more than my legs to get out. I will need an escalator. The Catholic Church is the only escalator to God."

Appalled at my skepticism about everything he held dear such as family, country and the spiritual quest, he insisted I read great books about the Catholic Church such as Karl Adam's Spirit of

Catholicism and the works of G. K. Chesterton. I didn't understand a word. I had absolutely no premises in common with these authors. However, I got a sense that there was a world of thought completely different from my own and that there was some kind of hope there.

One last intriguing experience before the time when Christ invaded my life in a way I could not dismiss as just a peculiar episode. Eva, a Jewish woman from my department at Johns Hopkins, loved art. I accompanied her to the National Gallery in Washington D.C. Actually, I hated going to art galleries of any kind, because my father used to bring us to museums as little children when we were too young for such long tours. I only agreed to visit this museum with Eva because she wanted to go so much and it was on the way to meeting some interesting young men.

Suddenly, I paused before the painting of Dali's Last Supper. I disliked the picture intensely from an aesthetic point of view and still do. But something about it drew me into the scene. It was the first time I had ever had anything resembling a mystical experience. I remained entranced for some fifteen minutes while time stopped. On a conscious level, I paid no attention to the content of the painting. I only wondered at the subjective annihilation of time that had taken place in front of it.

At Thanksgiving, I went home to New York City for the vacation. Totally by chance, my mother flipped on a program called *The Catholic Hour*. When she saw that there was an interview being conducted with two Catholic philosophers, she called me over to watch.

To my surprise, these professors, Dietrich Von Hildebrand and Alice Jourdain (later to become Dietrich's wife) were using words such as truth, love, and beauty. Instead of debunking such concepts, they were speaking of them with reverent conviction. On the spur of the moment, I wrote a long letter to them, care of the station, telling them of my search for meaning and my frustrations with my philosophical studies. This led to a meeting with Alice Jourdain, who lived but two blocks from our New York Apartment on 95th Street. That encounter was to change my whole life.

On the appointed day, I rang the bell of her apartment. The door was opened by her roommate, Madeleine Froelicher, now Madeleine

Stebbins, wife of Lyman Stebbins, the founder of Catholics United for the Faith. She has become a life-long cherished friend. Madeleine likes to boast that she was the very first among their large circle of friends to make my acquaintance. I was impressed by her warmth and cordiality.

She introduced me to Alice Jourdain. Alice, always called Lily by her friends, took both my hands, smiled, and ushered me into her room, extraordinary in the number of exquisite religious paintings and statues it contained. The most impressive thing about Lily then and now are her large, translucent eyes from which she stares out at people directly, never shifting her gaze in the slightest. This establishes an immediate bond. Her glance reaches right into the heart and soul of another.

Alice Von Hildebrand

In three minutes time, I felt that she wanted to share my anguish and would do anything in her power to relieve it. After some ten minutes of dialogue, she suggested that I might want to sit in on a few classes at Fordham University in the Bronx where Von Hildebrand and other excellent professors taught philosophy. Might I consider transferring there to continue my studies?

I grabbed at the idea. I think I would have tried anything she suggested, for I had the sensation that I was talking to a holy person: a long awaited guru, a woman mentor as powerful as Dostoevsky's Fr. Zossima.

I shall never forget sitting in on those classes at Fordham. I was accompanied by Stephen Schwarz, a philosophy student, who was the son of Professor Balduin Schwarz, one of the same circle of Europeans who had come over during the War in flight from Nazi persecution. Right away, I was impressed by the difference in atmosphere between Fordham and Hopkins. The professors at Fordham were interesting, vibrant human beings. They laughed boisterously in the halls. They lectured with fiery intensity as if the truth were a matter of life and death, as indeed it is.

Without further cogitation, I decided to risk losing my Wilson grant by transferring immediately to Fordham. As it turned out, the Chairman of the Department, Fr. James Somerville, S.J., called the Wilson Grant administrators and arranged to have the grant applied through Fordham.

When I returned to Hopkins to finish out the semester and to pack up, the faculty members were quite distressed. My fellow-students, in horror at the idea that I was leaving a marvelous university to lock myself up in the prison of Catholic dogma, insisted that I have a long talk with their favorite professor whom I had not yet met since he was on sabbatical. This man was a wonderful, warm Jewish intellectual, but nothing he could say in the two hours he spent with me could compete with the magnetism of going to a graduate school where the professors actually believed in Truth.

At that point, the God part had no interest. I was drawn only to the intensity of spirit I saw in the personalities of the Von Hildebrand circle. And yet, surely Christ was present during this transition, knowing that at such a center of intense Catholic wisdom surrounded by men and women who lived for Him alone, it would only be a matter of time before I would find Him and experience salvation at last.

The period that followed my admission to Fordham was a sort of honeymoon. The mornings I spent at home studying, happily lapping up concepts that could liberate. Then, I took the long subway ride from the 96th St. Station in Manhattan up to Fordham Road in the Bronx. Before classes, I liked to visit the medieval, stained-glass, Gothic-style library building, on the way passing the enigmatic, graceful statues of Mary — arms outstretched open to wisdom. How different from the architecture of Columbia University with its heads of the powerful masculine thinkers of the ages.

Then, on to the classes. There was the famous Von Hildebrand, a larger-than-life person. He was a coincidence of opposites. Having been brought up to spend half a year in Italy and half in Munich he had the gusto of Figaro but the mind of a genius: German in its thoroughness and synthetic abilities but precise and logical as an Englishman.

Von Hildebrand was a leader in the Christian phenomenological movement, a disciple of the early Husserl. He had converted to the Catholic faith from an agnostic Protestant background. To my amazement, he was able to refute the errors of skepticism and relativism, which paralyzed post-Kantian secular philosophy, in one lecture! If you want, you can read my summary of his arguments in the Appendix.

Dietrich Von Hildebrand

Besides the tremendous intellectual benefits of studying with Von Hildebrand, I was also attending the classes of Balduin Schwarz, later to become my godfather. A disciple of Von Hildebrand, his lecture style was more intuitive, inserting elements of pathos and poetry which touched other hidden chords in my soul. Balduin and his wife Leni, a convert from the same kind of atheistic Jewish family as my own, exercised a constant apostolate of hospitality. They often invited me to lunch at their apartment on 107 Street and Central Park West. They showered me with loving affection as well as giving me a demonstration of what a Catholic marriage might be like.

After lunch I often rode with Balduin Schwarz up to Fordham where he was to teach and I was to listen. These long excursions together on the subway became an informal introduction to Catholic sensibilities. I was astounded to witness Schwarz's disgust with the ads

Leni and Balduin Schwarz

plastered all over the stations and trains. He found it a despicable, demeaning of the human person, to display people as living only for beer or cigarettes.

Once this perceptive, highly sensitive man's dismay was focused on his own behavior. We were a bit late. In his haste to catch the local which came only at ten minute intervals, he had flung the coins needed for a token into the caged booth of the attendant. The black man within the enclosure looked out at him with a certain wounded look. He could see that he was being treated like a machine. My godfather-to-be caught that look. On the way up to Fordham he confessed to me the shame he felt at his thoughtless deed. What a revelation to me about the dignity of the person. This typical incident was but one of hundreds where I could see before my eyes what a difference it meant to have a conscience informed by Christ.

Later on, I would have occasion to study with the Jesuit Thomists such as Fr. Norris Clarke and Fr. James Somerville. Through their teaching, I came to love metaphysics and to understand the link between foundational philosophy and the mystical way.

Meanwhile, on the social scene, I was living a sort of double life. Mornings and afternoons were spent in the pursuit of philosophy, but evenings were spent with the last of my sinful boyfriends, an amusing, witty ex-philosophy major journalist whose alcoholism was fed exclusively by cheap beer at the bars we sat in for hours discussing ideas.

The summer after my first semester at Fordham found me in a conflicted state of mind. I could see that there was a truth worth seeking and I knew that moral values were real and objective. I vaguely thought that materialism could not be correct if there were such nonphysical entities as truth and goodness. But I could not see at all what these concepts had to do with the existence of God.

It was clear to me that my Catholic professors had qualities I had never seen among humanists — especially a love that was both intense and pure. They claimed that any goodness in themselves emanated from God, but God was just a word to me.

God, in His Providence, found a way to arrange for me to be able to receive more truth about Him in a manner that would undercut my intellectual barriers. It happened that Professor Schwarz and his wife were leading a Catholic art tour to Europe that year. As you recall, I was by no means a lover of art and certainly not interested in the Catholic part. Yet I hated the idea of losing my gurus for the whole summer, left only with life at the bar. When I was offered a scholarship for the tour, I accepted it with enthusiasm. (Later, I would discover that these funds were provided surreptitiously by Lyman Stebbins.)

When our tour group entered the Cathedral of Notre Dame in Paris, I burst into tears, overwhelmed by the spiritual beauty of this magnificent edifice. When the experience was repeated at the even more awesome Cathedral of Chartres the line of Keats came into my mind "Beauty is truth, truth beauty, that is all ye know on earth and all ye need to know."

And the pondering began. How could buildings so beautiful be constructed on the basis of superstition? What did those people believe who threw their hard-earned money into such building projects? Between sites, Balduin Schwarz spent the bus rides sitting next to me and responding to my questions. Once he searched through the boiling hot streets of Poitiers seeking a New Testament in English for me to read.

I had never even touched a Bible, believing it to be drivel as my parents had taught me. It was hard to understand, for a young woman used to reading either fiction or philosophy. After having perused the Gospel of St. Matthew, I fell into a deep sleep on the bus. God gave me a supernatural dream. I was standing at the door of a banquet table. At the far end were sitting Jesus and Mary. Mary beckoned to me and said in Hebrew "Come and join us."

Thinking back over this experience later, I decided that since I didn't know a word of Hebrew, Mary's use of it in the dream must have been a signal that Jesus was also for Jews.

Shortly after the dream, I had an impulse to pray. After all, on this tour I saw all these Catholics not only praying in the Churches we visited, but also getting up at the crack of dawn, observing the three-hour fast before Mass which still was required in those days, and kneeling in absorbed adoration at the Consecration where the bread and the wine were supposed to become the very body and blood of Christ. I used to go with them to these Masses and feel a sense of magnetism about the host.

I asked Balduin how I could pray when I didn't believe in God. He suggested the skeptics prayer: "God, if there is a God, save my soul if I have a soul." What a struggle it was the first time that evening to kneel on the floor and say that prayer. To an atheist there are few sights more repulsive than a person kneeling. Stand tall, head high, was the motto of children brought up on the poem "I am the master of my fate, I am the captain of my soul."

Right after my initial prayer, amazing graces started pouring out upon me. It started with viewing a simple unfinished sepia painting by Leonardo Da Vinci of the Nativity. To understand why I am sure that what happened came from God, you have to remember how much I disliked museums ... so that my consciousness was not one of welcoming interest but of bored concern with how quickly we could get out of the gallery to the delicious refreshments at the sidewalk cafes of France and Italy.

Glancing at the Madonna of Da Vinci, the entire beauty of the virtue of purity manifested itself to me. In a flash, I recognized that I had lost something I could never recover. Back at the hotel, I burst into tears of chagrin that there was an area where I could never compete with Catholics.

Da Vinci's Madonna

I had never told the Schwarzs about my sinful past. In the midst of my tears, I began to think it was dishonest to have won their love on false pretenses. If I was supposed to be so enamored of truth, how could I continue the deception? When I made my halting confession they threw their arms around me and showered me with love such as the father for the prodigal son or Jesus for Mary Magdalene.

Raphael's Christ

Another miracle connected with art occurred in the Vatican Museum. We passed by a rather faded tapestry by Raphael of Christ causing the miracle of the unexpected catch of fish after the Resurrection. All of a sudden, the face of Christ in this picture became alive! It was exactly like a living moving face!

The next day was to be our group's attendance at the huge audience of the Holy Father at St. Peter's. Now this, I had argued, was too much! How could an atheist want to see such a display of primitive adoration of some bejeweled figurehead out of medieval times? I made up my mind to spend the morning instead roaming about the streets of Rome. I reckoned without the Holy Spirit. Somehow my usually gentle professor Schwarz decided to demand that I go to St. Peter's to see the Pope. Astonished, I still protested but fi-

Finding Christ in the Catholic Church

nally gave in. I loved this man so much I didn't want to offend him about a matter that seemed so ridiculously important to him.

Jammed in with thousands of pilgrims joyfully waving handkerchiefs and yelling "Viva Il Papa" at the solemn Pope on his dais, I was not the least impressed. But then after the speech repeated in many languages, Pius XII, went down to the group of the crippled and the sick who were arranged in a circle to receive his blessing. My godfather-to-be, a short man of no special physical strength, lifted me up from the waist so that I could see the love of the Holy Father for his suffering sons and daughters.

And there it was. The expression on the face of the Pope bending over the disabled in sympathy was identical to the expression on the face of Raphael's Christ that had come alive for me the day before!

Now the fish was hooked. As a result of these special graces, I had to believe that there was something divine in the universe. In a peculiar manner, I had come to believe that Jesus was God before acknowledging there was a God.

On the other hand, I was an intellectual, not given to trust experience over reason. Upon returning to New York City, I rushed to the Fordham Library to find the books the Schwarzs suggested could give a foundation in reason for the faith that I had begun to accept very tentatively. About the Divinity of Christ, the argument that hit home was that of C. S. Lewis in *The Case for Christianity* (sometimes sold these days under the title *Mere Christianity*). Roughly, Lewis tells us that it is impossible logically to view Jesus as simply a great prophet or sage. Why? Because a mere human being who is a true wisdom figure would never claim divinity. Now it is clear that Christ claimed to be divine because that was what he was killed for: blasphemy in claiming to be God.

This leaves us with three alternatives: Jesus was a liar. Jesus was mad. Or, Jesus was who he claimed to be: the Second Person of the Trinity. Thinking Jesus to be a liar is incompatible with believing him to be the most ethical person who ever lived. Thinking him mad does not jibe with his transcendent wisdom and grace. That leaves one alternative: Jesus was God made man. So excited was I by this line of reasoning, I wanted to copy the book onto a stencil and send a copy to every non-believer I had ever met.

On the need for one true Church, I relied on Newman and Chesterton. For a person who longed for absolute truth, the idea of many Protestants I met that it made no difference which Christian Church you attended simply led me to shun their churches. If it was just a matter of taste, who needed it at all? I also read books by Jewish converts to help overcome the argument that the Church was evil as evidenced by the Inquisition, the Pogroms and the Holocaust[1]. You can read more about this in the Appendix.

In spite of all my intellectual and spiritual breakthroughs, something was still lacking. I longed to be a Catholic but I didn't seem to have enough faith to take the step. The moment of total conviction was a strange one. After a session with a diocesan priest in the Bronx who was giving me instructions in the faith, I was crossing a street on the way to the El train. On some unconscious level, divine grace took over. By the time I got into my seat on the subway, I had made my leap of faith, or rather, He had lifted me over the abyss of my fears.

On January 4, 1959 I was baptized at Holy Name Church on 96th Street and Amsterdam Avenue, the same church my father said we sat in out of curiosity as little girls. I had chosen Balduin and Leni Schwarz as godparents. The priest who baptized me was Fr. Damasus Winzen, the prior of Mt. Saviour Benedictine Monastery

---

[1] A summary of my own way of answering such Jewish objections to becoming a Catholic can be found in my book, *Tell Me Why: Answering Tough Questions About the Faith*, co-authored with Msgr. J. Pollard and published by Our Sunday Visitor. Readers from a Jewish background can also find much helpful information in the publications of The Remnant of Israel. Call (502) 325-3061 for free literature.

Finding Christ in the Catholic Church

(The whole Von Hildebrand circle were Benedictine Oblates). The devil had one last lick before the holy water was poured over my forehead. When Fr. Damasus opened the baptismal font a large cockroach in residence there scampered around the edge of the golden bowl. I was too frightened of making a mistake in the ceremony to scream.

After being baptized as Ronda Magdalena De Sola, I burst into a flood of tears in gratitude for being saved at last. Five years later, my twin sister Carla was baptized a Catholic and ten years after that, my mother was also baptized. Their journeys were different from mine. I firmly believe that non-believers are drawn to Christ and the Church by means of whatever their highest value was before. I came in through realizing that my highest value, truth, was embodied in Christ and the Church. My sister, such a lover of the beauty of music, came to know the beauty of Christ through classical masterpieces such as Verdi's Requiem.

My mother, who had always sought love, was given the grace to experience the hand of Christ blessing her with tenderness. She was also drawn by the love shown her by her mentors Fr. James Somerville and Beatrice Bruteau.

Later, my sister, who had studied at Julliard with Jose Limon, would leave the modern dance world to become a pioneer in the field of sacred dance. It began in a delightful way. On her way to a dance class, she passed a young man on a street comer who looked like a blond version of St. Francis, selling Catholic Worker magazines for a penny. Paul was a holy pre-hippie apostle. When Carla mentioned that she was a dancer, Paul asked her if she could teach him how to dance the Gospels as he had always had such a wish. A bold unconventional young man, as soon as he had learned a few steps, he decided that they should perform religious dances right on the steps of Catholic Churches. This, my shy introverted sister agreed to do under pressure of the awe she felt at the Franciscan joy and confidence of her new friend.

Sure enough, passersby gathered around to watch such a strange sight. After a simple dance, Paul and Carla would give witness talks to the crowd. In this manner the sacred dance movement was born.

For some months, Carla and Paul hitchhiked around the Eastern States without a cent in their pockets, dancing the gospels and being fed and lodged by fascinated townsfolk. Since this was in the very early sixties, their unusual brother/sister lifestyle surprised people but was believed. At that time "wandering minstrels" living without money were exotic but did not have the bad connotations later associated with the drug culture. Sometimes children thought they were seeing angels, for Carla, weighing ninety-five pounds and dressed in long, flowing robes dancing gracefully through the streets accompanied by her long haired partner, did look like an angel.

Carla and Paul went to Puerto Rico on a dance/preaching mission experiment, landing in La Perla, where they continued to dance the Gospel and live with the people. Since Paul had a strong attraction to the single life, he eventually took off on his own. Last heard of, he was with Vanier's L'Arche movement.

In the year or two he was with Carla, he managed to draw her out so that afterwards she could lead groups in dance in the most unexpected settings.[2] One of the most touching examples to me of my sister's leadership took place on an Easter Sunday in a park on the Lower East Side. The turf was divided between rival ethnic groups who never mixed. Inspired by the Holy Spirit, my delicate-looking sister coaxed the people to join a circle dance of praise to God.

Telling my story once again in this autobiography, I pause to thank my Jesus for bringing me to the truth. I realized with joy that truth was not a concept but a Person, The Word. And surely it was part of His plan that I should have been scorched by what I thought was love so that the abyss of my being would be wide open with space for the Divine Lover. Surely, it was also part of His plan that I should have tasted such closeness in my family that I could not be satisfied by the casual encounters of most academic life but would long for the solid form of community in Him I would one day find in His Church. As Augustine wrote: "Restless are our hearts until they find their rest in Thee."

---

[2] Carla De Sola Eaton has written several books about dance and prayer. *The Spirit Moves*, published by Sharing Company, *Learning Through Dance*, published by Paulist Press, and a new book, *Peace Rites*, from Pastoral Press. A fine video of Carla and her company, called *Dance-Prayer*, has just been made by Paulist Press.

Love and Marriage

I was searching for a holy, Catholic husband who would preferably look just like my adored St. Francis of Assisi. It never occurred to me that men who were just like St. Francis would not be looking for a wife but for the Franciscan Order!

Right after my baptism, I had two very close relationships with Catholic men, but one was too good and the other too bad. The one who was too good I rejected because somehow his very uprightness brought out capricious rebellion in me. The one who was too bad rejected me because he was looking for a saint and couldn't deal with my tarnished past.

Martin Chervin, my husband to-be, was the last person I would think God would provide. An atheistic Jewish businessman who was divorced!

Of course I would never have loved him if that was all he was. As you will see, he was a loving, seeking, man who would become a Catholic playwright and novelist whose works manifested the trenchant power and lyrical beauty of his mind and spirit.

Martin had previously been a seaman (second mate) and then a bookseller. It was as a sales manager at Vantage Press where my mother worked as an editor, that he first met my mother. My mother liked to tell her charming, sophisticated and literary friend Martin, then in his thirties, about her problems with her teenage daughters. Once he came to visit. After one look at me, he declared that some day I would be his second wife. He was married at the time to a modern dancer but on the verge of separation.

One day, while I was studying at Fordham, just before my European trip, I happened to be browsing in a thrift shop downtown called The Opportunity Shop. Suddenly a man approached me whose face looked familiar. It was Martin Chervin, on his lunch break. At that time he was sales manager of the trade department of Thomas Nelson, publishers of the Revised Standard Version of the Bible.

Now in his forties, he looked like the hero of a French movie with his quizzical sophisticated smile, roving, large, spectator blue eyes and informal sports suit. He asked me if I would like to go to lunch with him. In a scene that in a way set the stage for our entire lives together I replied "Oh, no. I have my peanut butter sandwich in this brown bag."

"Forget the peanut butter sandwich. It's probably stale. I know of a wonderful restaurant and you can have anything you like."

"Oh, no. I couldn't waste my sandwich. That would be wrong."

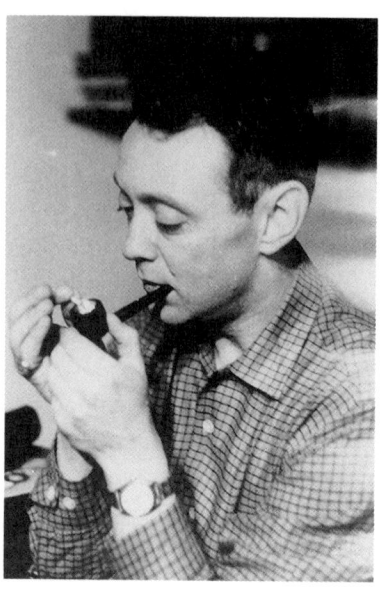

Martin, age 40

"All right. Come with me to my restaurant and you can eat your miserable sandwich while I have my delicious lunch."

Since then, I certainly have learned how to enjoy gourmet dishes. The part that stuck was the conflict between Martin's desire to get the most gusto out of life and my desire to do the right thing conceived of in terms of high Catholic ethical standards of a Franciscan type. One of the worst fights of our courtship took place in Paris when I refused to spend the first day on the Champs Elysee buying chic clothing, choosing instead to sit in the Cathedral. This seemed so contrary to Martin's idea of normal femininity that he asked me if I needed psychoanalysis.

Back in the restaurant in New York City, eating my peanut butter sandwich, I found myself tremendously attracted to this old friend of my mother. He asked me for a date, but I was just about to go on my Catholic Art Tour so I took a rain check. I think some other girlfriend intervened, because by the time he called again I had not only become a Catholic but had already suffered through the two relationships I mentioned above.

This time I was wide open to meet a man I could love, but I was very scared of Martin. It seemed to me as if the Devil was coming to get me. How could I even consider dating a divorced atheist roué? Well, just one evening out, far from his apartment, couldn't hurt...could it?

Martin recalls that I arranged myself in his Mercedes Benz so that I was sitting as far away from him as possible, almost out the window, spouting Catholic apologetics non-stop. I assumed he would be disgusted by my new-found faith and that would be the end of it. Quite the contrary.

Martin had been brought up in an orthodox Jewish home. He had been fascinated by the figure of Jesus ever since, as a young boy, he had read the New Testament in the Public Library. As a teenager, he became an atheist, as did so many young Jews of orthodox parents, first generation Americans. What he had not lost was interest in Christ. The picture of Jesus that filled Martin's imagination was the Jewish Christ as depicted in Rembrandt's portraits based on the Jewish men he saw on the streets of Amsterdam. Perhaps one of my ancestors?

On one of our early dates, we went together to the Metropolitan Museum of Art and stared at the most famous of the Rembrandt Christs for a long time. The fact that somehow the Jesus who I believed to be God was the Jesus loved by Martin, even though he did not know if he was divine, created a strong bond between us. (Later, when Martin started writing books with Christ as the saving personality, I always found his depiction not only compelling but inspiring.)

In this way, it turned out that my recent conversion, far from being a barrier to a closer relationship, became a bridge. Another plus was that he agreed immediately to respect my Catholic sexual morals.

Nonetheless, I felt very uncomfortable in his presence. I was worried about his previous marriage since I knew that Catholics could not marry divorced people. I didn't like the worldly aura that hovered about him with his expense accounts and fancy car. So, in spite of the strong attraction of his warmth, poetic, intuitive mind, and interest in Christ, I decided that I must find a way to get rid of him.

The quickest way I could think of was to invite him to meet the Von Hildebrand circle. Surely they would command me in the name of Christ to avoid fooling around with such a man and that would be the end of it.

To my stupefaction, they all loved him at first sight and decided to expend every effort to arrange for a dispensation from his previous marriage so that I could marry a man they thought would be a wonderful husband!

The approval of my mentors seemed to open the floodgates of love. After having so many tempestuous but tortured love affairs, I couldn't believe that any relationships with men could lead to true happiness. Yet here it was. In Martin's presence, I felt happy, sheltered, and free.

Since Martin was not a Catholic and therefore not under the jurisdiction of the Church, the matter of getting an annulment or dispensation was quite complicated, especially since his previous wife, the dancer, was a baptized though non-practicing Protestant. In those strict days, the New York Chancery turned us down, but suggested we might appeal to Rome with success. It happened that just then Martin had an offer to work as an international sales manager for Fawcett Publications, the company that provides American paperback books overseas, mostly for sale to tourists.

Partly because he loved the idea of traveling all over the world, but also because he could set up his base in Rome where we could pursue our marriage case, Martin took this job. We thought it would be a matter of some six months and then we could be married.

When it was evident Rome did not work speedily in such matters, I decided to leave Fordham, where I was pursuing a Ph.D., and move to Rome. For a short time, I lived cheaply in a rented room, spending my time in prayer, reading, and writing. As the case dragged on, I decided to take a secretarial job at an American oil drilling company managed by Texans.

Although the work was exceedingly dull and tedious, involving such feats as listening to Dictaphone tapes of men in Iran at the site reeling off specifications for rigs in fractions to be typed perfectly without the help of even liquid erasing devices, it provided a slice of masculine life I could draw conclusions from later in classes involving ethics of the work place. Two of the Italian secretaries, startled to see me rushing to daily Mass[1] during lunch hour with ten minutes left to gobble down a sandwich, took the opportunity to renew their own lives as Catholics.

A Benedictine Abbot, Fr. Gassner, also a canon lawyer, was appointed to handle our case. Every six weeks or so, I was to go to the baroque style office of the Italian chancery to check on progress. When I arrived wearing my chapel veil and carrying my daily Missal, they would put me off with lies about not knowing that Martin was in town to interview him or not having certain data which I knew had been supplied. One of the most frustrating moments of my life came two years afterwards when I was told by an American prelate that had I not been so pious or told them we were being chaste, they might have hurried up the case, as they always try to do for couples living in sin!

Between these hopeful visits, when I was still unemployed, I accompanied Martin on his fabulous trips through Europe selling paperbacks. The usual scenario involved pulling into a town in the middle of nowhere in Martin's little Sunbeam sports car. Before finding a hotel, I checked on the early morning Masses.

Next came the check-in counter of a hotel in say the French Alps. Martin asked for two rooms. The clerk is winking at him and trying to make it plain in deficient English that it is not necessary to have two rooms: "We understand such things." Then, Martin is insisting that I am not his wife and that we want two rooms. The clerk is shrugging his shoulders, looking at Martin as if he is insane and reluctantly handing out the two keys.

---

[1] I have never been able to understand how any Catholic who believes in the Real Presence of Christ in the Eucharist would not want to receive Him every day. As I wrote in the book *Church of Love*, now reprinted as *Signs of Love*, Holy Communion is Jesus' way of entering right into us in analogy to the way a human lover wants to get right inside. Unless a Catholic has tiny tots, no car in a rural area without buses, or no early daily Mass to go to, I think not to go is as sad as never kissing your spouse except on Saturdays.

On these long trips, we took great joy in the beautiful scenery, the lovely little towns, and marvelous cities. In between stops, I spent hours talking to Martin about reasons to become a Catholic. Mostly, I tried to get my points across by means of analogy to romantic love. "Can't you see that you need sacraments, not only prayer, just as in love between a husband and wife you need tangible expressions of love such as embraces not only thoughts going back and forth?"

In the courtship stage of most marriages, one can see patterns of closeness and distance. What always drew us together was love of beauty, especially as found in classical music. Even at the most difficult times, we could always sense our unity when listening to such works as Bach's *St. Matthew Passion*, or in a lighter vein the music of Puccini, Richard Strauss or Delius. We also loved to read books and enjoy foreign foods.

Tensions existed because our love for each other was, in so many ways, an attraction of opposites. While I wanted to soar spiritually into eternity and leave the earth behind, at the same time I was desperately in need of his love of life and appreciation of the human scene, sort of as a ballast. And at that same time that he clung to the earth, he also deeply loved my transcendent yearnings, sort of as a kite.

For two and a half long years, we waited for the resolution of our marriage case. One of the main reasons it took so long was because the Curial officials were hoping that Martin would become a Catholic. When a Jew becomes a Catholic, if his or her previous spouse will not accept Catholic life, under certain circumstances he is free by means of the Pauline Privilege to marry a Catholic.

Martin was much involved in his spiritual quest. From time to time, he had mystical experiences that would have converted many other people. Once, the large crucified Christ in the Jesuit Church of Gesu in Rome seemed to speak to him and tell him how much Martin needed His love. Another time, he watched an outdoor Mass in Brussels and when the people rushed up for Holy Communion, he felt drawn as by a magnet. Again, at a Christmas Mass at the Benedictine Monastery of Subiaco he felt divine grace so strongly that he rushed out into the snowy piazza to get away from the pull.

Love and Marriage

In spite of all these motives for faith, Martin refused to become a Catholic prematurely and insincerely for the sake of removing his impediments to re-marriage through the Pauline privilege.

During this time, we happened to meet a canon lawyer from Milan, a friend of one of our Italian lay well-wishers. He listened to our tale and told us there was no chance of getting a dispensation. Appalled, I went into the closet of my apartment which I had decorated as a tiny chapel and begged God to help me. While praying, I could hear the trumpet blasts of the Gloria of Bach's B Minor Mass playing on the phonograph.

It seemed as if all earthly happiness could only be had by marrying Martin outside the Church. But all eternal happiness lay in obedience. Suddenly, I got the grace to resolve to stay with the Church no matter what the sacrifice. Sadly, I told Martin of my decision. I am not sure he believed me. He thought we should wait for an official response from Rome.

A week later, we got the news that the canon lawyers in Rome had given us a Petrine privilege granted in cases where there are no children involved and where the first marriage would be annullable if one were Catholic. We fit under this because Martin's former wife had refused to have children. In Catholic marriages, there must be openness to new life. The Petrine privilege is called "in favor of the faith," signifying that the Church considers that the marriage will come to be something that will help the faith of all involved. Our document was signed by the famous Cardinal Ottaviani.

Our beautiful wedding took place on July 9, 1962. After all that long wait, here we were in what seemed like a Catholic version of a fairy-tale setting: the site was an old Church, San Onofrio, in the hills above St. Peter's of Rome, with a terrace garden replete with ancient fountain overlooking all of the city.

The wedding service, not a Mass since Martin was not a Catholic (in those days you could not have a Mass if it was a mixed marriage) was performed by a marvelous Camalodolese monk, Padre Benedetto Calati, with a long beard, dancing eyes, and a glorious personality combining profundity, solemnity and ebullient joy in the Lord.

En Route To Eternity

My mother came all the way from New York City. My godparents, Balduin and Leni Schwarz, came from Austria. The rest of the group were our few very dear Italian friends.

In spite of my euphoria at finally being able to marry my beloved Martin and the true smallness of the wedding, I managed to have the usual pre-bridal fits about details. I had a dream of a perfect white dress that would be utterly simple yet flowing. The dress was utterly simple but it wouldn't flow since the cheap satin could only come down in folds rather than in waterfalls.

Rome Wedding of Martin & Ronda

The wedding itself came off with splendid, sweet beauty. The small reception consisted of champagne, Italian delicacies and a wedding cake, following which we took off by rail for Brindisi, en route to Greece. The honeymoon was glorious in spite of the sweltering July weather and resulted in an immediate pregnancy.

Fortunately, the doctors in Italy are cautious about pregnancy. Even though there were no signs of miscarriage, I was advised to quit my job at the oil drilling company and relax. Since Martin was still required to make two month long European trips, it was decided by the seventh month that I should return to New York and stay with my mother where Martin would join me in time for the delivery.

The pregnancy was extremely tiresome with morning sickness way beyond the usual time, great fatigue and heaviness. I have a sad but funny memory of our first trip to Paris after the conception. On Martin's expense account, we were accustomed to patronizing the very best of restaurants. Alas, the entire gourmet meal, gobbled down only to be thrown up, found its final destination on the side of the curb outside.

I was also quite frightened of the delivery, my imagination having been fertilized primarily by Victorian novels with accounts of one out of two women dying in childbirth after excruciating pain. This was the very early days of the Lamaze method. It happened that my young ob/gyn Dr. Hassid, had written his thesis on the topic of natural child birth. Off I went to the classes, in those days somewhat exotic. It was only during the last evening's tour of the baby ward, seeing the tiny little infants in their cribs, that full joy broke out to overcome the previous nausea and fear. Something about the sight of these babies released the usual maternal instincts causing the most avid anticipation of motherhood.

With a month to go to the due date, I began to notice something surprising. When viewing my own protruding belly against the size of that of other expectant mothers I seemed to be much, much larger. Querying my doctor, I got no insight. I began to think I was going to give birth to a large giant.

Three weeks before the due date, Martin arrived from Europe. He asked the doctor if he would have time for a visit to his folks in Washington, D.C. who had not seen him for a long time. Certainly. Off he went, only to be summoned by phone in the middle of the night of March 21-22 to be told that his wife had been rushed to the hospital with placenta previa bleeding. So frightened was the doctor that he drove me himself from my mother's apartment to French Hospital. Once laid out on the long white hospital table, I began my Lamaze breathing. I seemed to have gone very quickly into what would be an approximately four hour delivery.

I was quite puzzled and scared by the appearance of not only my obstetrician but two others as well, who circled about my bed examining me. Through a haze of pain, I heard something about too many arms and feet. All the past literary images of death in childbirth recurred. I prayed very hard and announced valiantly that should it be a choice between my life and that of the baby they should certainly save the baby, whatever my husband might say.

And then, just as the transition began, there was Martin, dressed in the special father outfit, by my side with me shrieking my way without medication to the great moment when the little baby girl was born: Carla Maria Chervin. I was in too much agony to enjoy the sight. Later, I was told that even though Lamaze did not work in alleviating the pain, it had been essential because without that breathing and pushing I would not have been able to get a baby out fast enough to not have it drown in the placenta previa blood. Or at least that was how I understood whatever medical information was given me when I complained bitterly about the pain of the supposedly painless procedure.

Martin was beaming with joy, looking down at his first born. Then Dr. Hassid amazed us by instructing Martin with these words: "Don't leave yet, Daddy, there's another one on the way!" Six minutes later, there was a second little girl who would be called Diana Helen Chervin, my original name and my mother's name.

Exultant, Martin rushed down to the ground floor waiting room and embraced my mother yelling, "Helen, it's Carla and Ronda all over again!" So hard was that hug that it broke one of her ribs!

It was not Carla and Ronda all over again, for they were not fraternal but identical twins. And why had our doctor not told us that the baby was going to be babies? It turned out that they were the very first twins of this young Dr. Hassid. Before the days of ultrasound, it was not so easy to tell what was going on. He suspected twins, but not having heard two distinct heartbeats, he was afraid that one might be still-born. In that case, he decided not to announce it until he was sure it would live.

Our initial ecstatic delight was marred by the announcement that little baby Carla was having slight breathing problems and would have to be put in an incubator. One of the less than metaphysically educated mothers in my ward responded to my tears and incessant prayers with the thought, "I don't see what's bothering you. You were only expecting one, so what difference does it make if one of them dies?!"

This brought strongly into focus for me the absolute uniqueness of each baby even when "identical" physically to another one. Indeed, from the first moment of seeing Carla and Diana, I could sense differences that still manifest themselves today when they are thirty years old! Carla seemed the more delicate, winsome, and inward; Diana more friendly, buoyant and outgoing. When they were six months old I would dub little Carla by the pet name Pussy Willow and Diana, Dandelion.

Ties That Bind

Needless to say, delight in my darling little girls was not the only emotion that came with the change from being an adored young wife to being a mother. In the years to come, I would feel more and more bound by ties that were tight in unhappy as well as happy ways.

The negative part began simply with the physical difficulties of mothering twins. Since they were rather small, five pounds, ten to eleven ounces, the doctor insisted we keep them in New York City for at least six weeks before the trip back to Rome. What a routine. There I was, having never taken care of a baby more than once ... with twins! Both girls were extremely colicky. Not knowing what I was doing, I was sure that they would die if they didn't finish every ounce of each bottle. This led to a twenty-four hour feeding schedule, with one babe or the other drinking every one and a half hours for a half hour long drink. Sleep for me was obviously minimal.

It took me a long time to pay much attention to my own tiredness, so great was the joy in my little squoojels, as I called them. I loved to stare into their tiny eyes, seeming to see eternity in them, or as Wordsworth expressed it, each one "trailing clouds of glory." Martin was equally happy. He proclaimed that carrying the twins out of the hospital and pondering on the wonder of it all, for the first time he sensed how God the Father must feel about each of his creations.

The stay with the twin babies at my mother's house was the occasion of my first meeting with Martin's family. His father had died before I could meet him. His mother lived with her daughter, son-in-law and grandchildren in Maryland in the D.C. area. I took immediately to Annie, Martin's warm, loving sister and to Julius, called Julie, her husband, a large Ph.D. in physics, son of a Jewish immigrant ice-cream man who used to sell his wares on a tiny pushcart in Washington Square Park. Later, I would enjoy meeting Iris and Bobby, their children.

Martin's mother was another story. A short but large woman from the old country, Poland, she had a great heart but also a domineering will stronger than that of anyone I have ever met, save her son.

Later, when we moved to California she liked to visit for two months at a time partly to get away from "the bad weathers" back East but equally to see Martin's brother, Maurice, his son Ronnie, and our children. The only one in the family to retain the orthodox Jewish religion, she kept a kosher kitchen which she imported with her on visits. Feeling sad that her son Martin was reduced to eating *goyish* food, she would cook for herself and for him so that he would come to the dinner table to find a plate with two dinners on it, one made by his mother and one by me.

On her visits, Martin's mother also insisted on watching her soap operas with our children, finding it strange that we thought kid's TV should be monitored to include only programs suitable for young eyes. The poor, lonely woman, with nothing to do all day on these visits, naturally found it hard to give up her favorite entertainment, the soaps. She would try to sneak them in on low volume, one child under each large arm when we were not watching. This led to huge scenes.

While I was out working, Grandma Gussie also tried to help me by doing all the housework. I resented this as a slur on my own paltry efforts. It is too bad that all this happened when I was a fairly new wife. Years later I would have been delighted to have her perform all these services and laughed merrily at a double plate of food for my now overweight husband.

Gussie's fidelity to her religion was the one thing we had in common. In spite of being appalled that I was a Jew who had become a Catholic, she did respect the fact that I, like her, believed in following the law and daily prayer. Curious concerning what Christianity was about, but unable to read any adult books since her English was not that good, my mother-in-law snuck a look at the twin's little child-level books about Jesus. Happily, the one she choose was designed to do justice to the actual lifestyle of the times, the pictures being typical of Israel rather than depicting him as an

Anglo-Saxon god. After her research, my mother-in-law announced to Martin, "Now, I understand. Jesus was a good Jewish boy who was kidnapped by the Christians."

Finally after many years of visits, I had Martin tell her that even though I loved her very much it made me nervous when she made such long visits. Could she make shorter ones? She was deeply hurt and also furious. Since her motives were so loving, she couldn't understand how she could make anyone nervous. Her other pet peeve about me was that I was such a quiet woman! She is the only person with such a complaint about me. I realized that my constant prayers not to get into fights with her had led to a state of silence!

⁂

Soon after the visit of Martin's family to meet the tiny twins, it was time to begin the process of bringing the babies to Rome and trying to raise them in a foreign land. Our Italian friends had hired for us a young girl as an all-round helper, Maria. Informed that it was two babies not one, she immediately wanted more money. That was okay. I was happy to pay anything to have the luxury of two hour stretches between feedings for rest.

What I hadn't anticipated was how strange and lonely it would be for me, tied by bonds of love to my darling children, to be cooped up in an apartment with a teenage girl for two-month periods while Martin sold books all around the world. We had thought that with one baby we could take the infant and helper with us on those trips. With two it would be impossible.

My friends, some of whom also had new born babies, lived just a little too far away to make taking several buses with infants worth the fuss. From our apartment on the Via Gregorio Settimo, I would stroll them over to St. Peter's Square where the bishops and *periti* of Vatican II could be seen on their way in and out. Maria, the helper, went into a fit one day when I left her with the twins for more than the two hours between double feedings, while I went to check if it was black or white smoke coming out of the chimney to indicate whether a new Pope was elected. White! A long exciting historical wait with thousands of Italians and tourists to see Pope Paul VI give his first papal blessing. I believe it was during the two-month periods of Martin's absence that I was forced to deal with long stretches of loneliness for the first time. The desire to be close to a loved companion increased my need of church and personal prayer. I often think that had Martin been an extrovert, seeking daily conversations in depth, I might never have felt later on so great a need to teach and speak outside the home.

It is one of my favorite meditations to consider how many of the good things in my life came about because of lacks. We bemoan missing elements in our dreams of fulfillment with pitiful prayers of woe, and yet how often it is these crosses which open up into the fulfillment of God's plan with satisfactions we had never even fantasized about.

After six months of trying to live in Rome with Martin gone for such long intervals, I began to consider the idea of leaving our beloved Italy for New York where I would have my mother and sister and the Von Hildebrand circle as company while raising the babies.

Martin spent hours sitting on the balcony on Via Gregorio Settimo in deep cogitation about this question. In those days, it would not be hard to find another job in book sales, but it would be terrible to go back to the rat-race of Madison Avenue after the adventure of being a traveling book salesman with all of the world as a marketplace.

I think it was three days into the trip before I had a moment to stand out on deck and view the ocean. In a certain way, the disappointments and trials of this voyage marked the end of our happy time and the prelude to the many sad and terrible experiences to come.

※※

Bringing up babies in a New York apartment (ours was on 2nd Avenue and 17th Street) was less than ideal, especially if, like me, you hadn't a clue how to take care of little ones to begin with. The day started at about 7 A.M. with the little ones' cries. By 8 A.M., Martin would be off carrying huge laundry bags of stinking cloth diapers on his way to work. While the babies played in the pen, I would take care of household clean-up. By about eleven,

I was ready for the fifty steps to getting twins ready to go out to the park.

First there was the twenty minutes of dressing each infant in their heavy winter clothing, a process that could always require a complete replay if the baby happened to urinate or defecate during the dressing up. The dressing involved shoving the little arms and legs of one into the snowsuit while the other wailed at being without any attention. Then came sticking them into the playpen, and running down the three stories of the brownstone carrying the huge double stroller. Although it cost a fortune to rent, the apartment had no elevator.

Next came carrying the two heavy babies in my arms down the same flights of stairs, settling them in the stroller, holding open the heavy door with a shoulder while pushing the carriage out the door, for the short walk to the Church where I would take in part of the noon Mass by rushing in for the Consecration, then strolling the twins around the block, and returning for Holy Communion.

I recall once meeting one of my former philosophy professors at one of these Masses. I caught up with him outside the Church and wailed: "Nothing I ever learned in philosophy prepared me for diapers." When I had come out with the same complaint to the great Von Hildebrand, a man who had fathered only one son with his first wife, an old-fashioned German woman who did all the child care herself, he had replied with the less-than-helpful response "What's a diaper?" The professor I met this time, an American father of three, had a much better answer: "Stop reading Plato and Augustine and read Aristotle and William James."

When I spent a half year preparing for the comprehensive examinations, which entailed a review of the whole history of philosophy, I realized that he was right. Plato talks about the good, the true, and the beautiful. Aristotle about growth and motion. Children are good, true, and beautiful in essence, but in terms of daily life they are much more like perpetual motion. Augustine teaches us how to get to eternity through time, but William James, the radical empiricist pragmatist, teaches how to understand the material world and coping with one year old babies has a lot more to do with matter than with soul. Reading a biography of James recently, I was amused to discover that he found raising children so upsetting, that he found reasons to escape on long trips to Europe to get away! I guess all philosophers, even empiricists, have trouble with domestic life.

After receiving the spiritual strength I needed each day to deal with so much matter, it would be on to the square park of Second Avenue for the next few hours. This play area was visited primarily by skid-row characters and their refuse of cigarette butts and broken bottles. When the twins learned how to walk, they loved to pick up these butts and offer them to the half passed-out men on the benches.

In the middle of the two block long park was a small filthy sandbox in which some ten children at a time would be throwing things at each other while the mothers sat and chatted ruefully about the present and hopefully about their dreams of moving out to the suburbs. Once the twins were old enough to run around, unless they were willing to stay in the sandbox, it would be a matter of chasing two little ones in opposite directions to make sure neither ran onto the perilous street full of killer cars.

I loved the time in the park. Unless it was pouring rain, I was always there for this was the time to relieve the monotony of child raising by talking to other adults. It was at that park I was to meet Emily Pechefsky, a Ph.D. in literature from Columbia University whom I still love and visit twenty-nine years after. She came to the park with her little Rebecca.

By 2 or 3 P.M. even the most intrepid of us mothers were ready to stroll our dirty little tykes home for baths and naps. Having developed the siesta habit in Italy, I always used this time for sleeping. Then came preparations for dinner amidst the squeals and fights of the twins and then, at last, the lovely moment when Daddy came home. A hectic dinner followed by Martin with one baby on each knee exercising his fictional talents by making up long amusing serial stories for them, different episodes every night.

I always made sure the twins went to bed early so that I could have time to read while Martin played music on the stereo.

In spite of adoring little Carla and Diana and finding them cute and lovable beyond all expectations, I simply hated the binding tasks of mothering. I would spend hours brooding about how odd it was of God to think it good to have so many years of helpless dependency for young humans. Then I would picture in my mind how someone could invent a tube that could connect their little bottoms to the toilet avoiding the miseries of diaper changes.

I had not the faintest notion how to discipline children. We had been brought up fairly permissively, but because both my mother and father had themselves been raised strictly, they still had some sense of boundaries. I had none. Instead of stopping my little ones from throwing food out of their high chairs onto the floor, I would sit and try to figure out whether table manners came under the rubric of ethical absolutes to be enforced no matter what, or rather only under the category of customs which made no difference. While I philosophized to myself about these weighty concerns, the floor was becoming littered with mounds of disgusting thrown-away tidbits.

By the age of one and a half, little Carla and Diana were running the house and I was hiding behind the kitchen gate weeping. All my friends and mentors told me that I was just not suited for full-time motherhood. "Go back to school, finish up your Ph.D. and get a job!" they would advise. Oh, no. Not idealistic Ronda. Since I had decided that the only way to keep a husband and be a saintly mother was to fulfill my feminine role to the hilt, it was unthinkable that I should give up and adopt the career lifestyle of women like my mother who were neither happily married nor holy.

By this time also, I was beginning to feel unhappy about the way *my* little darlings had ousted me from my role as *the* little darling. Having married a man twenty years my senior, I had lapped up all the lavish fatherly love Martin was happy to give me. But when the real children came, they became the princesses and I felt like the maid, Cinderella.

Whereas before the twins came I used to be called Ronushka and other treasured pet names, now they were called by the diminutives and I was simply Ronda, or sweetheart, mostly when something was wanted. (Eight years later, when our son was born, I could understand the change in Martin better. Here was this miniature version of everything I had loved in my husband — fresh, without annoying complexes, longing for my love.)

Another feature of those days was the impact of my sister's Franciscan lifestyle and activities, which filled me with envy and admiration. I began to question our middle-class lifestyle and wish I could also pursue, if not so radical a trust as to go off on trips without any money, at least simplicity and generosity to the poor. This yearning, kindled by my sister's spirituality, led to conflict in my marriage.

I thought that anything not a necessity belonged to the poor, as is taught in the Encyclicals of the Popes. Martin believed God wanted us to enjoy everything He had made available to us. He also had a distrust of charities springing from street-wise New York City, where everyone knew that men with donation cups took seventy-five percent for themselves. Fortunately, Martin went to a lecture given by Mother Teresa of Calcutta. Convinced of her holiness, he agreed that we could tithe her works.

Seeing how miserable I was becoming in my *hausfrau* role, my friends persisted in their schemes for liberating me. They drew my attention to a special grant for mothers who had a hiatus in their education and wanted now to go back to get their graduate degrees. Reluctantly, I filled out the forms. I managed to win one of those Danforth fellowships that would take care not only of tuition but also of baby-sitting fees for two years.

Back I went to my beloved Fordham University to finish my course work by taking classes once a week, then studying at home for the comprehensives and finishing with a thesis on the philosophy of the religion of Kierkegaard. I loved being back in school. When I left to go

Diana and Carla Chervin

Ties That Bind

Carla

to Rome to pursue our dispensation, I didn't think I would miss Fordham. Now, not an alternative to securing a husband, but a respite from child raising, it seemed a wonderful place to be.

Soon, we decided to make the big move to buy our first house out in the suburbs, where the twins could play in a beautiful garden. We selected a charming house, surrounded by birch trees, in the area of Spring Valley in Rockland County over the bridge north of New Jersey. At this time, Martin was working for his own company called Books Abroad, commuting into New York when he wasn't off on trips around the world, this time shorter ones so I would have more emotional support at home.

Diana

This was the time of holding the twins close, one under each arm, reading to them, writing down their cute remarks, enjoying their radiant beauty and teaching them to love the God who created the nature around us. But living in the country had a difficult side as well. To get to Church or to go shopping, it became absolutely necessary to learn how to drive. A zero-sensate person with no sense of machinery, I failed the driving test three times in the midst of hysteria on my part and raging insults on my husband's. After finally passing the test by a hair, it would take me another five years to be able even to change lanes on the freeway. My strategy was to hug the slow lane. If this disappeared suddenly to become an off ramp, I would stop the car and wait with lines of enraged motorists beeping behind me until there was a space of at least ten car lengths for me to maneuver back into a lane. During these times of frustration, I would weep and curse.

The next worst aspect of suburban living was the lack of a park at which to meet other women. Each of us had our own one half or one acre park in our backyards. I did become friendly with other mothers on the block, but since many of them were really into housework it was usually I who had to admit to being stir crazy with my twins and had to beg to come over to talk to them.

It was during this time that two really tragic patterns developed which would throw my life into crisis for many decades. Under the strain of living in the United States with its tense, success-oriented, business mentality and our draining commutes, the communication between Martin and myself began to break down. For example, one summer he sent us off to Fire Island with my mother for a few weeks while he stayed at the office in New York, coming out for weekends. I missed him terribly and couldn't wait to return to be with him. When he suggested we stay an extra few weeks, I was heart-broken. How could he stand to be without me?

When other things happened that I could not understand and thought were unforgivable, I withdrew entirely, instead of working it out, deciding that my marriage was fatally unhappy and that I should take refuge in God alone. Looking back, I wonder how the next twenty years would have been if I had insisted on confrontation, forgiveness, fresh starts, and greater communication instead of retreating into a sort of private spiritual cell.

In the light of the Marriage Encounter movement, it is startling to me that someone so talkative as myself never grasped the concept that it was more important in a marriage to talk not about ideas but about the most vulnerable hurts and feelings. I notice that most women of my generation had the same disastrous blind spot. We just assumed you swallow pain rather than dealing with it, although in my case, it came out in rage at the twins. I often find that born Catholic women are shocked by my casual use of words like hate and rage. Most Jewish and Italian women think nothing of expressing themselves in such strong terms. To give a clear picture to readers, when I use the word "rage" do I mean to convey that I spent every moment of the day screaming and throwing things around the house? Not exactly. I mean that I spent lots of time growling inwardly and then yelling when something would push my buttons. I would say I used to average one fit a day. (My daughter Carla tells me that it was not the number of times I yelled at them that was upsetting but the edge of hysteria which gave them the impression that any moment I might go insane!)

Faced with my conviction that my marriage was doomed to resigned misery, I remembered my contemplative Jewish convert friend Charles Rich, the only person who ever thought I could be a nun. He is a man of soaring mystical prayer who had converted from a Jewish background himself.

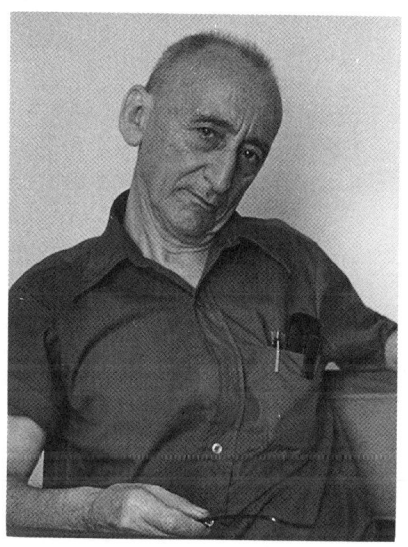

Charles Rich, 1960

A man of strong intuitions, Charlie had his own ideas about the future of his new acquaintance. His first words to me were "Do you want to be a saint? If not, I don't want to bother to get to know you." Bewildered but delighted that he thought I could be a saint, I became perplexed after a month or so when he added that he thought I was destined to be a contemplative nun.

Now in my grief over my failing marriage, I went to visit him in New York City and asked him to recommend ways of prayer and reading that could lead me on a fast path to holiness. He warned me that reading celibate spiritual sages such as St. John of the Cross can be misleading for married people. I insisted on my need to find a means to arrive at a union with Christ close enough to assuage my deep hurts and proceeded to devour the Carmelite mystics.

In a way, this path was good for me. Without giving up my previous idol-worship of my husband, I might never have gone as deeply as

I did into the spiritual life. On the other hand, my absorption in prayer created a much greater barrier between myself and Martin. If Jesus was my true love, who was Martin? In my bitterness, I was sure of the answer. Martin was my cross.

Actually, at the time when the tensions between us became so dreadful, Martin hardly noticed the change in my feelings. The reason concerned the second tragedy that befell us at that time. At age forty-nine, with no previous history, my husband developed nearly fatal asthma. It began with allergic attacks leading to use of inhalers, then increased to a deadly loss of breathing functions with emergency trips to the hospital and strong doses of cortisone.

I did sympathize with Martin's sufferings, but mostly I was just terrified. Having absolutely no knowledge of medical realities it was stupefying to have to deal with daily attacks. Worst was having to make judgments about whether to call for an ambulance when my forceful husband insisted he didn't need anything. "Just let me try to relax." Those who are themselves asthmatic or who have close family members with this condition are all too familiar with the anxieties this ailment causes both to the patient and to the family.

Frantically, we tried to remove everything in the house that could cause allergic asthmatic responses. When this didn't help, we thought of moving to a climate less cold and rainy than that of New York. At first we thought of Arizona or Palm Springs. After a few visits to these places, which I thought incredibly beautiful, Martin, with his seaman background, announced that he would rather die than be so land-locked.

Eventually, we moved to Los Angeles, California, where Martin's brother Maurice, and his family lived. Trying to avoid smog, we bought a townhouse in picturesque San Juan Capistrano, Martin setting up a branch of his business nearby.

After a year of struggles with nearly catastrophic asthma attacks, Martin's brother heard of a plan for a six month visit to the National Jewish Hospital in Denver specializing in diseases of the lung. Here, they cut out portions of his sinuses, arranged for suitable doses of cortisone and other medicines and taught him how to be more relaxed during attacks.

Ties That Bind

It was lucky I had earned my Ph.D. When it became clear that Martin could in no way continue to run a business, he was forced to an early retirement, and I into full-time teaching as a philosophy professor. The story of my experiences as a teacher, speaker and writer will be the subject of the next chapter. Before closing this one, I want to let my readers know that if I had my twenties to live over again I would have immediately sought out a Catholic counselor at the time when things began to get so unhappy. Then when Martin became so sick I would have joined a support group for families of the chronically ill.

Why didn't I make moves that would seem obvious to me today? Hindsight is not always too objective, but I think it was because I was too spiritually proud to look into remedies which would mean confessing weakness. I wanted to prove that I could overcome all hurts and difficulties by becoming a saint. And, at that time, being a saint meant needing no one but Christ. I do believe, even now, that there have been saints, Benedict Labre, the wandering streetperson holy man being the one that most readily comes to mind, who truly were sustained by Christ alone. Most of them, however, leaned very heavily on the human-to-human support of mentors and spiritual friends.

May God and my family forgive me for my part in extending sufferings that might have been healed more quickly had I been humbler.

Family 1984

Defender of the Faith

As soon as I became a Catholic, I wanted to defend the faith day and night. This I was able to do in three roles that opened up to me in my thirties: professor, writer, and lecturer.

Most graduate students do quite a bit of part-time teaching before getting their Ph.D.'s, either as teacher's assistants or earning a living by means of high school teaching. I was an exception.

The main reason was my fear of being at the other end of the anti-teacher feelings most students exhibited in my days as a student. I realized I was quite different in loving school and teachers so much. Fearfully, I postponed the leap to the other side of the desk until I had all my graduate work behind me.

Truly, I had more time to write my thesis with twins of two and a half years old than most of the other scholars. Whereas most of the men were working full time as teachers, then going to class, and arriving home to help their wives with the children, I had four mornings a week free, with the twins in a parish baby-sitting cooperation I helped organize (we had fifteen mothers, each one sharing one morning with three other Moms in exchange for four days off), and then four hours at night from 7 to 11 P.M. Watching my daughters let their babies stay up until ten and eleven at night, I am amazed they can stand it. I was recently boasting of my well planned free time with two year olds when my daughter Carla remarked that she still remembers lying awake for hours after a goodnight prayer, not the least bit sleepy, imagining terrifying things that could happen in the dark. Alas!

In any case, right after getting my Ph.D., I was offered one course in evening school for adults at Fordham University Extension. It was scary driving an hour at night with my dreadful automotive skills and scarier still to face a class for the first time. However, after five minutes of lecturing, I knew this was it. This was the profession I had always been meant for. Talking, discussing, questioning, just as I had as a child in our loquacious home, and as I had as a student, but still better because I WAS IN CHARGE!

I had authority to plan the course, to figure out how to engage the students in dialogue, to bring in delicious tangents of my own devising to spice things up and to relate classical truths to the daily experience of these wonderful adults who came at the end of a long day's work trying to get a degree, overjoyed to find that they were also finding truths that might change their lives. I loved it and they loved it. When we moved to Capistrano I actively looked for part-time teaching.

⁘⁘⁘⁘⁘⁘⁘⁘⁘⁘—❖—⁘⁘⁘⁘⁘⁘⁘⁘⁘⁘—❖—⁘⁘⁘⁘⁘⁘⁘⁘⁘⁘—❖—⁘⁘⁘⁘⁘⁘⁘⁘⁘⁘—❖—⁘⁘⁘⁘⁘⁘⁘⁘⁘⁘—❖

The year Martin went to the hospital in Denver saw the beginning of my full time work at Loyola Marymount University of Los Angeles. Loyola, a Jesuit University, and Marymount, a college administered by the Marymount Sisters, had just merged. The all male philosophy department was looking for a female role-model professor to round out the staff.

Happily, Dr. Jasper Blystone, the chairman, had a fascination for Edith Stein, the Jewish convert disciple of Husserl who had ultimately become a Carmelite nun and martyr. When I arrived for the interview as a Jewish woman convert, disciple of Von Hildebrand, who had studied with Husserl, he saw me as an extraordinary living exemplar of this seemingly unique Stein.

The twins were six years old in 1969, when I began full-time teaching. They were in first grade at the Mission school. I arranged for them to be picked up at 2 P.M. to visit neighbors. The drive from Capistrano to Los Angeles was more than an hour and then another hour for the return trip, and I usually arrived home at around 4 P.M.

In spite of fatigue, I have many happy memories of my daughters from that time. Both girls endeared themselves to me with their sparkling joy in life, mischievous cuteness, and depth of interest in understanding life, precocious for that age. In Diana's case it took the form of remarks aimed at logical consistency; in Carla, of poetic intuition.

Characteristically, Diana sought to win others to her by her fun-loving ways and Carla sought closeness with emotional intensity. In a few year's time, these traits would express themselves in Diana's impressionistic art and Carla's poetry which gave us so much joy.

※※※

The first day of class at Loyola Marymount, I cried all the way home. I had given my well-planned lecture in introduction to philosophy to some thirty young people. Based on carefully typed notes from previous courses, I was sure it was good. The students seemed happy enough.

During my office hours, an attractive student, Eddie Baguio Adcock came walking into my office grinning from ear to ear. "Come now, Dr. Chervin, don't tell me you plan to just read from those old notes for a whole quarter? You don't even know who we are or what we think yet. Why don't you come in tomorrow without any notes and see what happens?" I nodded meekly, jumped into my car and wept. I would have to quit. That was certain. I had never seen a single college professor operate without notes. It was like being asked to arrive naked.

A morning person who begins to sink after noon, my brooding got worse and worse as night fell. Martin was far away in Denver. I didn't want to bother him. Even though he has always been a terrific person for giving good advice, asthma had become an overwhelming concern. Lying in his bed surrounded by other patients perhaps breathing their last, I couldn't see making a long distance call to ask whether I should resign after the first day at Loyola Marymount.

After early Mass and an hour of prayer in the car on the way back to Los Angeles I got the strength to give it a whirl. Never a quitter when it came to intellectual challenges, I decided I would just lay it all out to that class. Tell them about the tears and tell them we were going to try something revolutionary at the suggestion of their classmate Eddie.

Well, it worked. I became Ronda Chervin, a person on fire with truth who wanted to know and love my students, instead of Ronda Chervin, teacher in the image of my own favorite mentors of the past. Professors like Von Hildebrand and Schwarz also loved their students dearly, but in class they kept to the tradition of giving wonderful lectures with occasional questions and answers.

What I was led to do was to open everything wide, get the students to share their deepest reflections with their peers, impart to them not only the truths of Catholic philosophers but also witness to them how these concepts shaped my own life, not only in the past but ongoing each day as it unfolded. For a few years I even photocopied a journal of my experiences and ideas to hand out once a week.

In a very short time, I had a following of eager students[1]. The students loved to come over to the house and play with Carla and Diana, who adored them. In the midst of their skeptical doubts about the faith and about their own path, these young people emerging into adulthood just at the end of the hippie era were hungry for truth and love. I was too young at thirty-three to be a domineering mother figure they would have to reject, but old enough to be a sort of Pied-Piper for Christ, leading them back into the Church many of them had left. Mostly it was the young men who had left, and their girlfriends who needed a woman in authority to back up their often weak attempts to keep out of sin.

Among the young people who liked to dialogue with me were three monks from St. Andrew's Priory at Valyermo who were finishing their undergraduate work at Loyola Marymount. Brothers Gregory, Francis and Thomas soon got me interested in becoming a Benedictine Oblate of their monastery. I loved to visit for a few days just after the end of a semester. Here I could be free from all my roles and drink in the graces of peace that so many lay people find at this beautiful priory, now an abbey.

Among the many professors I was close to, the one who gave me the most support was a professor by whom the College became known, Frank Sullivan. This man became something of a father

---

[1] The names of some of these students are Craig Fellin, Bill Vallicella, Ken Bower, Tina Anderson and her friend Kerry, Eddie Baguio Adcock, Joannie Beingessner and her friend Patti, John Pearring who would marry Joanne, Karen Bangs, Michael Cronin, Andy Snella, Dave Ryan and his friend Chris, Nona Monteverde, Michael Healy, Jim Harold, Jim Glasson, Greg Erlandson, Kathy Hall, Rick Salazar and many others. Special love to you all.

figure for me, and his death in 1975 was a time of great grief for me.

By February of 1970 Martin returned from Denver, still chronically ill but no longer in imminent danger of death. The transition was hard for both of us. The time at the Jewish Hospital was for him a contemporary version of Thomas Mann's Magic Mountain refuge for tubercular patients. He had felt safe with doctors and nurses at immediate call, surrounded by others who had been through the same shattering experience of having become semi-invalids through the ravages of asthma. Now he was returning to the normal world with the care he needed in an emergency twenty minutes away.

He would learn to cope with his disability by means of taking up the career he had secretly always wanted to pursue, that is, becoming a full-time writer. He embarked on a colossal project — to dramatize the forty days encounter between Christ and Satan in the desert by constructing a dialogue between them spanning the major themes of the Old Testament. What was Satan thinking when God created the world? And how would the Second Person of the Trinity defend the Father against the charge of having created so flawed a hybrid in man that no good would ever come of it?

To a woman as religious as myself, who also valued authorship more than anything else on earth besides the Mass, and who had come to love her own profession as a teacher, there was no question but that I would affirm my husband's writing plans and be happy to shoulder the main burden of financial support of the family, aided by his disability payments. Later on, some friends who thought that being a career-Mom was a tragic error, asked me why I didn't go on welfare rather than consent to leave my children for most of the day. The thought never occurred to me. Middle-class people simply didn't go on welfare. Besides, I was doing something I loved and the children had the benefit of a father at home willing to talk to them endlessly, telling them stories or listening to their prattling. I can only remember one person, a writer himself, who ever suggested that it was a fine noble deed on my part to be willing to work full-time enabling my husband to write without worries about income.

In fact, although the outcome of a lifestyle invented because of Martin's illness did enable him to pursue his cherished artistic goals as novelist and later as playwright, this was not my main motive in continuing to work full-time. Once I realized how much I loved to teach, I could devote myself to it in the spirit of a crusade. By that time, there was so much confusion in the Catholic Church that defending her by means of Christian philosophy became truly a courageous heroic endeavor. Spiritual energy for this apostolate was greatly increased after being prayed over for the release of the Holy Spirit.

This came about in quite an astounding manner. My sister was visiting from New York during the time Martin was in Denver. She started talking to me about glossalalia. What? "You know, speaking in tongues, as in the Acts of the Apostles." I was convinced that my dear twin had flipped out. She quietly persisted in her witness, finally asking me what my present relationship to the Holy Spirit was like. For once without a word to say, I realized that I had no personal bond with the Holy Spirit at all. He was just the end of the Glory be. The Son I adored. The Father I believed in from a distance, but the Holy Spirit was nothing to me.

One evening, after the girls were in bed, I was playing for her the Bach B Minor Mass, the same piece that had been so powerful at the time I thought I had to choose between the Church and Martin toward the end of our Roman dispensation. When the record came to the blaring magnificent "Cum Sancto Spiritu" of the Gloria with the lights dim, my sister's face started glowing with light and changed into the visage of the living Christ — a cross between El Greco's and Rembrandt's Christ heads.

Quickly, I whispered "go ahead with whatever you want to do." She laid hands on me and softly prayed for the coming of the Holy Spirit. Immediately I started praying in tongues, which I had never heard before, and a fiery praise-filled joy bubbled through me together with prodigious fresh energy for teaching.

Shortly after, I joined the fledgling group of Catholic Pentecostal students at the University, led by Fr. Ralph Tichenor, one of the soberest Jesuit theologians of Loyola Marymount. At that time, when so many faculty and students were suffering from doubt about the truths of the faith, it was wonderful to find myself at prayer meetings surrounded by Catholics whose beliefs had been kindled to red-hot enthusiasm by the Holy Spirit. Some almost fainted with awe at the Consecration of the Mass, many lined up for hours for Confession. Instead of arguing about transubstantiation, these Catholics knew the Real Presence first hand.

Another joy that came with being part of the prayer group was that the release in the Spirit seemed to make Catholics more like Chassidic Jews. Like my remote ancestors, who swayed and prayed aloud, charismatics moved about raising their hands and shouting out their praise to God. I felt that I fit in better with people who were so enthusiastic and excitable. Scoffers insist that this way of prayer is too emotional. I disagree. I wrote a book called *Why I am A Catholic Charismatic* defending the expression of emotion in worship. Even though deep silent reverence is a great tradition which needs a place in every service, so does joyful praise. Should we all look like corpses just at the moment we are enunciating lines from the Psalms such as "Clap your hands with joy all ye peoples!" What a relief to come into a church and weep if I was miserable, knowing my sisters and brothers in the Lord wanted to know I was suffering so they could pray over me.

⁂

The graces of the Holy Spirit soon led me into speaking, first in the Los Angeles area and finally as far away as Germany and Australia. At first, I wrote out every word of these talks, then went on to making an outline and finally to mostly speaking directly, heart to heart. In every case I spend quite a bit of time in prayer before a talk and love to have the sponsors pray over me that my words may be truly from the Holy Spirit and reach out to whoever is suffering most in the audience (I believe I have succeeded if the most closed looking person I spy at the beginning is smiling or crying by the end).

I also began to publish small and then larger books. (A list of these titles can be found on the back cover of this book and more about some of them is in the Appendix.) I credit my progressive secular education with the ability to write freely and quickly. Many Catholic friends with much greater ability than I simply cannot overcome the tyranny of the high ideals of their early classes in composition. They truly believe that anything not rewritten endless times and honed to perfection should never see the light of day. By contrast, I was trained simply to express myself. I can write as fast as I talk, if not faster.

As a life-long idolater of books, it was a tremendous happiness to be an author. The best of all is to meet people who tell me my books helped them through times of trial, leading them to the comfort of Christ's love.

Didn't I ever sit still and have fun? Yes, indeed. My hobbies during this time included crossword puzzles and knitting. Of course, the way I did these things was a bit compulsive. By the time I gave them up I would have to finish a puzzle book a week and I would knit not just on a couch but constantly, while talking to people, and even in the dentist's chair. The best things I ever did in knitting and crochet were custom-made afghans and blankets for the family. On our tenth wedding anniversary, I made a huge bedspread with high points of our life depicted in different wools sewn over the knitted panels.

To return to my narrative of my early years teaching philosophy, after one year of commuting during the time of Martin's stay in Denver, we moved from Capistrano to a house at 7612 Cowan Avenue, about a mile from the University. Now the hard part was not the commute, but the combination of worry about Martin's asthmatic emergencies and the heavy load of household chores after I came home from school.

Although before I started teaching I had no problem with cooking since it was about the most interesting and varied of household tasks, once my energies were absorbed in the challenge of academe, trying to concentrate on tasty meals, plus laundry, dishes, etc. became unbearable to me. At that time, Martin, having gown up with a typical Jewish Mama of the old traditions, thought it was practically a sin for a man to enter the kitchen. He would take care of all matters concerning major purchases, bills, repairs, etc., but none of the daily drudgery.

I would manage to grind my teeth and offer up in prayer the cooking and cleaning, but then, after the house had settled down I wanted to relax on the couch and mark papers. There were enormous quantities of these because I had the students doing creative workbooks of my devising which they would hand in each week for my perusal. Somehow all the simmering resentment would erupt when about 9:30 P.M. Martin would ask me to prepare coffee and dessert for our late evening snack. Why couldn't he do that small thing for me, I wondered as I seethed with rage — not unexpressed anger but volcanic explosions first at coffee time and then spilling over to just about any request he made at any time of day. This developed into an unpleasant and highly painful split between happy, buoyant, pseudo-strong Ronda the professor and miserable, nagging, tired Ronda of the home; a tension that was to become even more severe as I neared the mid-life transition of forty.

But way before that painful time, came our miracle. Between the birth of the twins, my thirty-fourth birthday, and Martin's fifty-third, I had three miscarriages, two of them called hydataform moles, which I understood to be not a fetus, but rather cancerous growths developing around the embryo, evacuating itself by means of miscarriage. Perhaps this is not an accurate explanation (I have had one more mole and two more regular miscarriages, for a total of six).

Although I certainly felt sorrow over these unborn babies, it was nothing as bad what must be felt by parents who have no living children or who don't believe that their miscarried or still-born children will be waiting for them in eternity for an eventual reunion. As I used to say to a friend, Gabriel Meyer, who was picked beforehand as godfather to some of these miscarried babies, perhaps his prayers rendered them so holy that their feet never touched our sad earth.

This past history of unborn babies made the advent of little Charles Paul seem like a miracle. In the womb he also gave signs of miscarriage but somehow he managed to hang in and was born into the world prematurely on October 20, 1971. He was only four pounds and twelve ounces just below the weight where babies can leave for home. He was required to spend two weeks in the preemie ward where I visited him twice a day to start him on breast feeding.

Charlie was my first child to enjoy this boon. When the twins were born it was still not the mode to teach mothers how to do it. At

Daniel Freeman Hospital in Inglewood, the nurses patiently worked with me the whole two weeks it took before Charlie learned how to suckle. As my baby son snuggled close, gazing at me with his pure soulful eyes, he illustrated the line from the Psalms: *"Yet thou art he who took me from the womb: thou didst keep me safe upon my mother's breasts."* (Psalm 22:9)

Charlie was an extraordinarily happy baby. He was to function in the family as a sort of miraculous source of fulfillment and solution to long-standing problems. For my husband Charlie was Isaac to his Abraham, the unexpected son who would eventually act out my husband's life-long passion for music by becoming a cellist and a composer.

For me, Charlie was a reconciler as well as a challenge. Since this successful birth followed closely upon a session where the famous healer Fr. Aloysius of the Claretians had prayed over Martin for health and faith, Charlie also seemed a sign of a happier life for us in our marriage.

He was also easier for me to handle because, since I was teaching most of the day, he went to the house of a grandmotherly woman who took in children from nine to two. Then my dear student Kathy Hall, a Catholic artist, would take him a few hours in the afternoon while I took a nap.

Let me share a few "snapshots" of Charlie's early years: his favorite book was Little Bear, illustrated by Maurice Sendak. I read it to him more than a hundred times. His next love was Batman. As a tot, he liked to dress up in a makeshift costume of this hero and run around the house shouting "Batman! Batman!" By six he was writing novella-long fiction about old-fashioned knights battling with fantasy demons.

Here is one excerpt of his early style: "Jesus came down to earth for eight days and the world came to his mass. 'I have come again, hell is gone, so is the devil, so is the demons. Satan is an angel again.' If Satan can change into an angel then you can turn into a saint. THE WORLD MUST CHANGE. Try. Try. Try. ..."

Eager to make sure that my son would not become an effete egghead, I insisted that he be allowed to play with the kids on the block, join Little League, and later practice Tae Kwon Do. He had a riotous fun-filled youth with his friends Mark and Greg.

Little League was less than successful. His first time at the plate the announcer quipped "Charlie Chervin is feeling very confident, he doesn't even need a bat!" But at martial arts he was terrific. I signed him up for a group of University students because it was free and convenient. The group was led by a black, born-again art student, Tyrone, who mingled intense coaching with readings from Castenada. Others in the group dawdled over the reading assignments. Charlie read these tomes at a clip of one a week. Soon he became a mascot of the older college students. He was especially adept at inventing his own patterns. At Tae Kwon Do he went as far as earning his brown belt. Tyrone left Los Angeles and the group dispersed.

Music was Charlie's first love. Although having superior talents in writing, he thought it was better to work in music, piano and cello, because there was even more beauty in it. This was a hard decision. Because of his premature birth, he had rather poor hand-eye coordination.

From boyhood, he manifested a spiritual nature of the prophetic type. His favorite religious movie was *Brother Sun and Sister Moon*. St. Francis was the saint Charlie wanted to emulate. An interior soul, he liked to ponder life around him in terms of Christian values. He had a great desire to help us to grow. Here is an example. After a family quarrel, Charlie was berating me about my faults. Annoyed I remonstrated "Hey, why don't you work on your father and your sisters for a change!" His reply: "Oh Mom, you're the only one who's humble enough to listen to a child."

Another time, I asked his opinion about a dispute I was having with Martin concerning money, with me, as usual, advancing the Franciscan viewpoint. Pushed to take sides, Charlie told me: "Well, Mom, you're always right, but you say your ideas in such a nasty tone of voice that no one will ever accept it."

He once came, because I couldn't find a sitter that day, to a workshop I gave on prayer, Charlie remarked afterwards: "Gee, Mom, that was terrific. If you ever did any of those things you talk about, you'd be a saint!"

En Route To Eternity

A tremendously successful and happy kid in junior high at a magnet school for music and the arts, the first year at high school was rough. Crossroads was a prestigious private school for music students. Most of the young people came from Asian-ancestry families where children had practiced on their instruments three hours a day from the age of six. When Charlie was not accepted in the orchestra, it was his first major experience of failure. The second year, they let him in but he was still behind. He made one or two close friends but felt awkward among the "in-group" of already professional level musicians. In his pain, he took refuge in reading Shakespeare, Dostoevsky, Steinbeck, and Tolkien.

Noticing how depressed our bright, merry Charlie had become, Martin took him out of Crossroads and sent him to Hamilton High, a Public School with a magnet program in music. These two years were among the best in his life. He enjoyed the inner-city atmosphere of many cultures and flamboyant cultural traits. Since many of the students were beginners, Charlie quickly ascended to the top in the classical line. It was here that he met creative teachers who fostered not only good technique but also his originality. At the graduation concert the students performed Charlie's Suite based on Tolkien's *Lord of the Rings*.

During the last two years of High School Charlie made the friends who were true soulmates: Athan, Jessie, and Chris — a painter, an actor, and a writer. He also came to love a beautiful, petite, Chinese-ancestry singer and dancer, Joyce Lui.

Unlike the twins, whose teenage rebellion was spectacular, at first Charlie's seemed rather mild. He became gruff and sarcastic not only with Martin and myself but also with his sisters with whom he had been exceedingly close. Carla used to talk to him for hours a day and write poetry for him to set to music. It was a blow to him when she married, and even more when the first son was born, replacing him as the youngest son of the family. Diana's first born, Jenny, was different because she was a girl.

A psychologist who gave us counsel told us that he was typical of what Jungians call "the eternal child syndrome." Such youngsters refuse to become adults, identifying all meaning in life to the free-spirited joys of childhood.

Mid-Life Crisis and Amazing Graces

It was only after reading a book by Levinson about adult developmental psychology that I realized that what I considered to have been a special personal crisis was typical of the struggles of people around the age of forty.

What was happening in my life surrounded the apex of that mid-life transition spanning the years between 1974 to 1978. Let me start with what was going well for me. Charismatic prayer, speaking and writing, and little Charlie, who was moving from adorable little boy into fine school boy. Even though I had as much difficulty disciplining him as I had with the girls, because it was part-time mothering, it was less stressful. I was especially happy with Martin's joy in his son, lightening the heaviness of chronic illness.

Otherwise, things were getting worse and worse. Carla and Diana, as children, had been our pride and joy. Carla wrote exquisite poetry and Diana was a painter. At least once a week, we would be relishing some product of their creativity. In character, Carla was tender, intuitive, empathetic, and giving. Diana was bubbly, analytic, and extremely friendly. They were as religious as most children, willing to engage in home traditions I would devise for them and able to pray from the heart.

Although at first fiercely jealous of little Charlie, they soon settled into a playful and mothering attitude toward him. His arrival meant that they quickly had to assume a more helping role in family life. Carla, who had the talent of a gourmet cook, took over the preparation of dinner and Diana did setting and clean up. They also had to change diapers when I was not around.

By age thirteen, just before my mid-life crisis, the twins were beginning to manifest signs of rebellion. Aside from the normal difficulties of adolescence, one reason for stored up anger had to do with their feeling that they did not fit in well among their schoolmates because they had us as parents.

Not as different as myself and my sister, they still seemed and felt pretty alien to the majority of Los Angeles kids both in public school and in the Catholic schools we sent them to for junior high and high school. Diana now asks why we didn't move to Venice Beach, the hippie area near Loyola Marymount where family eccentricities such as painting the house bright green among all the beige and gray ones would have been less conspicuous. She was surprised at the simple reason. The houses in Venice cost a fortune compared to those in Westchester where we settled.

In spite of all my time-consuming efforts to involve all three in "normal" activities such as Camp Fire girls (like Girl Scouts), Little League, Tae Kwon Do, I could not exempt them from the feeling of being different. They felt that we had not prepared them for a world which scorned the values we held dear; that they had no cushion for the culture-shock of a society that held conformation to a strict norm above all else. Actually Carla and Diana seemed popular enough to me. They always had close girl friends and did well in school, qualifying for the gifted program.

When they were thirteen, we sent them back East to Martin's family who owned a condo at the beach in Atlantic City. That summer marked the transition. Picking them up after the summer at the airport, I happened to run into a sister I knew. While waiting for them to emerge from baggage I was chatting with my friend about my marvelous daughters. "Oh, here they are, I can introduce you to them!"

Bounding toward me came two girls I could scarcely recognize. It wasn't only the tiny mini-skirts, makeup, and costume jewelry they were sporting but also a kind of brazen look that said "We escaped from your world of Catholic values into the exciting mainstream, and you're not going to stop us!"

By seventeen they had dropped out of high school and began what to us was certainly a roller coaster to the bottom of the pits. I promised my daughter Carla I would not describe in my autobiography the tumultuous wild life she led between fifteen and middle twenties during which time we lived in perpetual fear and rage. My daughter, Diana, on the other hand, says she would not mind my writing about this period in her life.

Mid-Life Crisis and Amazing Graces

Briefly, right after dropping out of high school with a High School Equivalency Test, she started working full-time at a donut shop in a supermarket. After a few years of that, we persuaded her to take the GED and try Loyola Marymount. All children of faculty get free tuition. She did so brilliantly on the GED that they let her in. After a week's time, she quit. She hated the unfriendliness of the students and the stiltedness of formal classes. Neither of my daughters has ever gone back to school, both claiming that it is a hateful atmosphere.

Although promiscuous, Diana did not get pregnant for quite a number of years. Happily, we made the acquaintance of a Jewish convert, educational psychologist, Joel Rakow, with a Ph.D. from Harvard who had started a small company making training programs for computer operators. He needed people who could do word processing. Diana and Carla applied. Within six months, Rakow realized that he was dealing with young women of talents far beyond simple word-processing. Simple, huh? It took me five years to master word-processing myself! Soon, he had Diana doing telephone sales and Carla writing programs. In a more sophisticated form of the same work, Diana now makes roughly twice my salary with three years of high school her only formal education!

Unhappy relationships of love led to a suicidal episode with an overdose of sleeping pills. The doctors who pumped out her stomach told us it was a bluff. I will always recall Diana afterwards lying on our bed with Carla, her twin sister, holding her for hours trying to persuade her to rely on our real love instead of fantasies about the love of the irresponsible man she was seeing.

Humorously, but maybe also gracefully, Diana's first pregnancy came after I had gone through a long prayer of healing of memories. The book by the Linn brothers, I believe, included a section about miscarried babies. The authors pointed out that sometimes daughters will be infertile because of grief for their miscarried brothers and sisters. Readers were advised to name each of these babies and say prayers for them. I thought I could never think of six names, but in fact they came rolling out of my unconscious at waterfall speed. Immediately after this, Diana told us that she was expecting a baby. Although she was in love with the father, neither of them thought they were suited for marriage.

En Route To Eternity

Carla Chervin Conley

Peter Conley

Diana moved in with us for the last period of pregnancy and gave birth to the beautiful little girl who is our first granddaughter, Jennifer. For a while, they lived with us, but then Diana left to live a more independent life, having Jenny taken care of during work hours by a mother doing home daycare.

Both my daughters, now thirty years old, are happily married to men we love. Peter Conley is Carla's husband and Pete Jump is Diana's husband. Each family raising two marvelous offspring, our beloved grandchildren: Jenny, Nicholas, Christopher and Alexander. As is characteristic especially of identical twins, they married two guys who knew each other well, having been roommates. Alexander and Christopher were conceived in the same month in the wombs of Carla and Diana. Since Alexander came early, he was able to be

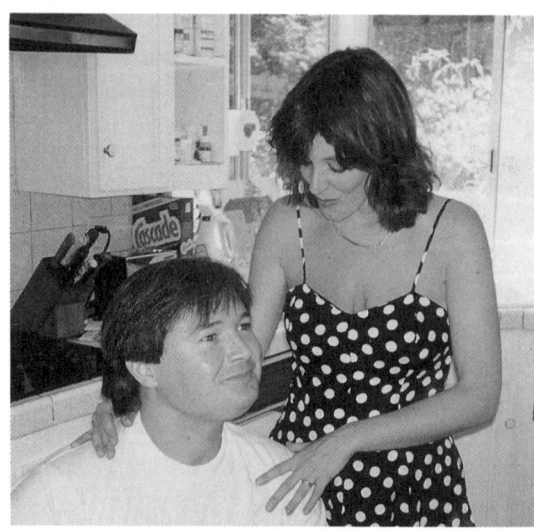

Diana and Pete Jump

present at the birth of his cousin. They seem like little twins when they visit.

Before writing about my grandchildren's personalities, I want to say a bit more about my present relationship to my daughters.

For the last three years I have been living with my daughter Carla and her husband and children in an extended family home in Woodland Hills, California. Such close proximity has brought about many healings. On the one hand, present-day attitudes trigger off bad memories of the past, leading to fresh battles. On the other, there is such a flow of mutual affection and deep love on a daily basis that this far outweighs the negative crises. I especially enjoy watching her maternal gifts flourishing — such a fine mixture of delight, understanding of the individual feelings of her sons, and dedication to their needs.

My daughter Diana lives about an hour away. Our best times are when we go out together, far from the others in her family, for heart-to-heart talks. These encounters seem to be allowing the insights she is getting from psychological counseling to filter through many barriers. She is greatly fatigued from working full-time, very successfully, with the joyful but also heavy duties of child raising. I am happy to see her begin to spread her wings as a writer. I watch her ripening into a mature woman — responsible, deep and searching.

Our first grandchild, the only girl so far, is Diana's Jenny. Of partly Scandinavian ancestry, Jenny looks like a blonde princess. With long, straight hair, hazel eyes, sometimes grave, but with rowdy, vivacious movements. Like her mother, she has lots of artistic talent. She is old enough to take in some of what I tell her about God.

Jenny

En Route To Eternity

Nicholas and Alexander

Nicholas Martin Conley, Carla's first boy, now three and a half, is my elf. Fiercely masculine and a lover of super heroes. I love his merry, large, black eyes, knowing and amused.

Next to be born after a terrible bed rest pregnancy for Carla was little Alexander Charles, now one and a half. He is a little love, a creature of melting, bubbly, sweet responsiveness. His cousin, born at almost the same time to Diana, is Christopher Charles. He is an adorable baby, already showing signs of being a rock of sturdy strength with a love of life.

*Martin
and grandsons*

*Alexander
and
    Christopher*

1993

One of my most piercing sorrows is that Diana and Carla to this date do not participate in the sacraments. They left church-going during their wild years, occasionally seeking out confession or very sporadically attending church with us on big holidays, but never on a committed basis. They believe in God and know how to pray, but they have no personal use for those ways which Jesus invented to get so close to us that we call the sacraments. They did have their babies baptized and will let me have them prepared for Holy Communion. Please pray for them.

Mid-Life Crisis and Amazing Graces

Back to my multifaceted mid-life crisis. Worrying about my daughters during their teens and feeling myself bereft of a close community of Catholics, I dreamed of moving into some tight group such as a charismatic covenant community, one of the leaders of which was then our closest family friend Gabriel Meyer, or into the Third Order Dominican Community of Jewish converts called St. Martin de Porres, some members of which are Jewish converts of the Remnant of Israel directed by Fr. Arthur Klyber. Such fantasies could never materialize because Martin hates communities.

Tensions in Los Angeles when my daughters were young were also heightened by my mother's move from New York to live near our family. Although she knew she would have difficulties with me and with Martin, she loved Carla and Diana dearly. Having little to do, she drifted into hanging around Loyola Marymount, sitting in the cafeteria talking to students and auditing classes, particularly in the philosophy department where she had a natural entree through me. Since she always sided with the viewpoints of the dissenting members of the Church and since I was running a crusade against such views, our relationship degenerated even more than it had before. I regarded her as a traitor to the faith and she regarded me as a grim fanatic.

Diana Chervin & Helen DeSola

Before long, acquaintances were amused to witness us yelling at each other in hot debate along the pathways of the University, especially after Sunday Mass at the student chapel. On the one hand, I wanted to cut her off completely. On the other, my Catholic principles, and the admonitions of my spiritual director, ensured that I should try to break through in love and especially not deprive my mother of her happiness in being close to my daughters.

The climax of ill-feeling came when I was having lunch with her and with Gabriel Meyer, our friend, then a charismatic leader; now a novelist and journalist. I love this great family friend for his warmth, perceptiveness and charm, his brilliant insights into Church and society. I hoped that if my mother could be released in the Holy Spirit, she would become more pious and our relationship would improve. Over pizza and wine, I grew more and more angry when I realized that she would use the time with the leader not to listen to his wisdom but to relate her usual amusing anecdotes of the past. Noticing that he was enjoying it as much as she, a feeling of fierce hatred filled my heart.

Walking her home to her apartment afterwards, she suddenly fainted in my arms in a heart attack. The paramedics came immediately. I called Gabriel, who was a healer, and he came to pray over her. The doctors told me she had a eighty percent chance of dying. I sat in the waiting room, praying up a storm, feeling exceedingly guilty about the hate I had felt that might have operated like voodoo to cause her attack.

When she recovered, we started talking about putting into effect a long-time dream. She would build an addition onto our house so she could enjoy the grandchildren and be close enough to help in emergencies. This turned out to be a disaster. Filled with hope in the beginning, once ensconced she could not stand the noise of the boisterous girls and little Charlie's boyhood revelry. It was even more painful for her to be living so near me and yet unable to really talk.

Exhausted by my usual overload, I had no energy at all to try to overcome the ideological and emotional difficulties with my mother, who would continually goad me with her sharply differing ideas. I felt rejected because she refused to affirm me as a professor, a writer and speaker, making carping remarks such as "Well, you're a housewife with an intellectual hobby," or "I'm glad you found an outlet for your little tracts," in response to the little books I was publishing. She felt rejected because I refused to affirm her about anything, seeing her as a woman with a terrible past who refused to be healed by grace, reinforcing others in the same sins I was trying to preach them out of.

Annoyed at my mother's nagging about the noise, Martin told her she should move out and that we would rent her wing and give her the proceeds. Once she left, however, he started thinking that any tenant might object to the noise. In a formal, legal manner, we agreed to pay her off monthly the $10,000 she had put into the addition.

Talking casually to a Sister about my past life, she suggested that it was a great pity that my father had never met his grandchildren. She was sure that no matter what the reasons for rifts in the past, any seventy-year old man would urgently want to see the children of his children.

(As described earlier, after the separation, my father communicated with us only through my grandfather. However, at age twenty-one, thinking myself an adult who no longer had to put my mother's ideas first, I decided to make contact again. This led to a trip to San Diego to visit the home of my father and his wife Dorothy. It was an important reunion for me. Dorothy was most eager to make a friend of me, especially since she was rather lonely, my father's usual skill in making enemies leaving her without as many friends as she, an extremely gregarious woman, would have enjoyed.

Now comes the tragic soap-opera. I encouraged my sister to make a healing visit herself, knowing that she had been much closer to my father than I as a child, and assuming that it would be a great thing for her to be reconciled as well. Just before her trip out West, I enclosed my wedding photographs as well as hints about how to deal with Dorothy such as "She has a real inferiority complex about her intellect in comparison to our mother's. She isn't very interesting, but she's bright enough, so be sure not to rub her the wrong way on this." Or, "She prides herself on her cooking. It is very good but somehow heavy as lead."

Once arrived in San Diego, my sister accidentally left this letter wrapped around the wedding photos in plain view of Dorothy who read it and naturally reacted with hysterical misery. My father viewed me as a two-faced Judas and in spite of my effusive apologies, cut off all communication with me, though continuing to write occasionally to my sister.)

It is easy to see that this Sister's suggestion of reopening the relationship was quite a challenge. I called him and we arranged to meet at a restaurant near Sea World where we would take the children first so that in case he and his wife rejected us on sight, we would not feel we had wasted the day. The whole time in Sea World, I scanned older men's faces, sure that my father would come there secretly to spy on us before the later afternoon date at the restaurant.

I was shaking with fear when we walked up to the Fish Market Restaurant in the Marina in San Diego, holding the hands of our children tightly. My father looked delighted to see us. Dorothy, to my great relief, simply winked in a charming, inviting manner.

To continue with elements in my life which at this time caused me psychological tension, my sister married a fascinating nurturing man, Arthur Eaton. An Episcopalian psychologist, Arthur had interests ranging from meditation, homeopathic medicine, and Native American culture to politics and gourmet cooking. With a deep appreciation of my sister's work combined with a desire to nurture her through affection, food, and help with the myriad details of running sacred dance companies, he has been a source of much happiness.

Carla DeSola and Arthur Eaton

My relationship to Arthur has been rather stormy. Although I love his *joie de vivre* and kindness, I disagree with most of his ideas about ethics and theology. I am grieved that since her marriage, my sister has been less faithful to Catholic teaching and practice than before. (It is not really that I am so narrow-minded as to be unable to love anyone who differs from me in his or her philosophy of life. I have several very close friends of opposite ideas on certain matters who remain very dear to me. The reason I can overlook these sources of conflict is that these friends, knowing how strongly I stand on issues such as pro-life, don't goad me into argument. Arthur is too much of a crusader to keep his opinions to himself. As the Jungians insist, it is often people who have traits similar to our own who rattle us the most.)

As you will see in the last chapter, my negative feelings would be modified by the love and empathy he extended to me at the worst moment of my life.

In the meantime, things at the University were no longer as rosy as in my description in the last chapter. As the hippie era gave way to the affluence-at-all-costs seventies, I had less and less students in my classes who were interested in alternate lifestyles based on Catholic ideals. Many of the students openly admitted that their goal at Loyola Marymount was to party for four years and then get a good job afterwards. Naturally, such students were hardly eager to listen to a philosophy professor, in a required core course in ethics, urging them on to chastity and social justice.

One guy told me that, right in the clinch, his date proclaimed "No further! I'm a disciple of Ronda Chervin!" A young woman who openly cursed me in class, later admitted that my narratives about a pre-med student rationalizing an abortion were exactly the same as her excuses and that I made her frantic.

Some key faculty members and priests seemed to me to stand on the other side about matters of crucial importance to me. The feeling that my initial popularity was giving way to resistance on all sides, combined with the lack of affirmation I experienced in the family, led me to lean more and more heavily on men at the University who seemed both powerful, loving, and understanding.

I had too deep a need to be surrounded by communal love and harmony to easily dismiss rejection by others on the job. As compensation, I tended to develop sometimes overly intense bonds with the few who agree with me.

It might have helped me to confine work outside the home to part-time, keeping the family as the base. Working full-time, I readily fell into the trap of substituting work friends for family. Of course, it is easier to get along with friends seen for a few privileged hours a day than to struggle with the total personalities of the family. One spiritual director of mine remarked wryly that the only cure for infatuation is marriage.

I found it extremely difficult to confine work relationships within boundaries. I wanted allies to be real friends and friends to be available not only at lunch time. During the time just before my crisis, certain friendships at work left me with feelings ranging from joy, to fear, to dread. Given my background of loss of my father, the worst emotion with regard to male friends was terror of being abandoned. At any moment, some cherished, indispensable ally might reject me or leave the University.

I believe that my stress came from a combination of factors: my girls reaching the age of wild teens; my mother's exacerbating continual rejection; seeing Dorothy, the beautiful, feminine younger woman of the past who won my father from my older mother; the growing problems of acceptance of my ideas by faculty and students at the University; and my loneliness in marriage to a man who seemed on the verge of death every day; all contributed to the climax of my mid-life crisis.

This painful time I now view as a desperate attempt to live out the softer, more playful, girlish side of my nature through closeness to people with whom I didn't have to be mother, career woman, or crusader.

The immediate cause of my mid-life crisis came when a close friend abruptly cut off the friendship. The loss of this friendship led me to a point of suicidal, hysterical misery. The first day of this crisis, I felt abandoned by God. Since I went to daily Mass, prayed a half hour a day in chapel, and kept up a running dialogue begging Christ to save me from everything evil or disastrous. How could He have let this happen?

Then something wonderful happened which has always made the song Amazing Grace dear to me. It seemed as if Jesus swooped down, enfolded me in a tight embrace, and proved to me that his love was total and merciful. No matter that I had been on the verge of chucking him out in favor of extravagant dreams of escape from all my crosses. His love depended not on me but on his own overflowing heart.

Right after the agonizing break with my friend, I went to the Priory for a retreat. Father Gregory, my former student, heard my general confession and mirrored for me that intense love of Christ for my poor, battered heart.

As one of the signs of His saving love, Providence arranged for me to start serious psychotherapy with a marvelous elderly Catholic woman, Andree Emery, a member of a Secular Institute — women who are consecrated to Christ but who live in the world in terms of dress and profession. Andree, originally from Hungary, was a brilliant, creative woman of vast empathy and insight. Amusingly enough, there had been a time in her life when she had been married to a Communist leader in New York City. One of the topics of conversation had been how to get rid of that Ralph De Sola who was informing on them to the FBI!

In a subtle, round-about way, she began to deal with my psychological and spiritual problems. Essentially, she was convinced that the main difficulty was an inflated belief that I must look like a saint to ratify my role as a Catholic Crusader instead of humbly admitting to my limitations. Why did I have to cook dinner for teenage girls and a husband who lived at home? Why not admit my duties were too tiring and that I needed more help from the family? Wouldn't it be better to more assertively look for more justice in my life rather than building up huge resentments while imagining that any moment I would become my image of a saint who could make any sacrifice out of love for Christ no matter how unnecessary?

Shortly after my therapy began, Martin decided that he would become a Catholic. Nothing could have given me greater joy or opened the door to renewal of our marriage more than this step. No matter what the quarrels going on, that kiss of peace at Sunday Mass would bring us peace. Around this time, Martin's writing bore more fruit. His beautiful play *Myself: Alma Mahler*, about the marriage of the composer Gustav Mahler, was performed on a stage at Columbia University in New York City with Judith Barcroft playing the lead in the one-woman show. Most of the family accompanied Martin to New York. It was glorious to see the members of the Mahler society eating it up. This play has recently been performed on numerous stages in Arizona by Pamela Fields.

He also started writing a pro-life play called *Born/Unborn*. This project developed partly out of Martin's frustration with tales of pickets and rosaries in front of abortion clinics that I insisted on participating in. Martin was convinced that it was necessary instead to fight the media war by presenting a play that could reach the heart.

Another extraordinary grace came at this time in a touching manner. I was at a charismatic healing service. In the midst of the many physical healings the leader called on all the married couples to stand and raise their joined hands while making an act of total forgiveness of each other for all past sins and injuries. Feeling so alone since my husband disliked charismatic prayer and never came with me to such events, I started to cry. Then I got the grace to grab hold of my wedding ring and make the same act of forgiveness. Afterwards it occurred to me that worse than my husband's weaknesses in the eyes of Christ might have been my many years of non-forgiveness.

On arriving home, that husband who never went into the kitchen, looked at me and said, "You look tired. Would you like a cup of tea?"

I figure that for the first time in years, he was looking into the face of a woman who was radiating forgiveness instead of hate, and this released the love in his own heart which he claims he has always felt.

This was not the end of spectacular graces coming at the end of my mid-life transition. One day in 1980, a woman of our parish who was a member of the Blue Army of Our Lady of Fatima asked me if I would like to have a statue of Our Lady in my house for Christmas. Truly, the idea was not particularly appealing. No one in my family but myself was into Marian devotion. It might get knocked over by the dog. My own bent was toward charismatic prayer and liturgy of the hours and even though I prayed the rosary every day faithfully, I was not much into special devotions such as surrounded prayers for the intercession of Our Lady of Fatima.

Thinking, however, that my Blue Army friend Ruth Sullivan was one of the holiest women I knew, I decided I ought to let her bring the statue. After all, who could refuse to have Mary come for Christmas?

I had imagined the statue as rather small. Instead, in the door came Ruth and a friend with a velvet box the size of a child's coffin. Reverently they set her up on a table and then handed me a booklet of some twenty pages of consecration prayers. It is important to the rest of this story to insist that I said these prayers with them without the slightest enthusiasm, just as a formality out of politeness.

Immediately after the women walked out the door, blowing a kiss to their holy mother, sublime peace like a blanket fell over my whole body, irritable soul, and restless heart. Stunned, I lay down on our bed to pray. Even though I had thought of my prayer life as perfect because it flowed so continually with charismatic graces, this was still all within my own will. In most cases it was I who decided to pray and then God would send the graces. Now, it had changed. It was Christ who was taking the initiative, flooding me with quiet joy. By night, this supernatural content was augmented by interior visions, one after the other. By morning, it was clear. Mary is not just our mother to answer our petition prayers. Mary is the archetype of contemplative mysticism. She saw Jesus face to face and she wants us to be as close to him as we will allow.

Supernatural illuminations seemed to be poured into my soul together with an outflowing of spiritual prayer-poems. I was touched to find that my husband loved these poems which he helped edit, although generally he finds my writings too didactic for his literary tastes. It seemed impossible, though, to tell him about the interior feelings and words from God that led to the poems.

I wondered who I could tell about such graces in detail. Immediately, I thought of Charles Rich, the Jewish convert mentor I described earlier who had spent forty-five years of his life as a Catholic mystic.

Sending him letters about my experiences led to a daily correspondence for some ten years. His letters to me I have edited under the title *The Holy Dybbuk*, published by St. Bede's Press. For the story of his beautiful and unusual life, see his Autobiography and my biography called *Hungry for Heaven*. Drawing closer to him by mail and bi-annual visits in connection with speaking engagements near New York City, where he lives in a Jesuit residence, led to a true spiritual friendship.

The fatherly love of this holy man expressed in letters for so many years was to be one of the prime ways God chose to heal me of the wounds of my own father's leaving me when I was eight.

In the Appendix are some of the more striking passages in the letters I wrote to him which constitute a diary of Christ's special graces to me during this privileged contemplative period of my life.

This manner of intense experience of God in prayer continued on every day for about two years and then slowly faded out to be replaced by a sense of wordless union. From that time until 1991, my prayer life remained on a kind of plateau punctuated by special visions such as seeing the sky opening to reveal a new heaven and a new earth at Medjugorje.

It would take the most terrible tragedies to bring me into a different sense of Christ — one where my only prayer would be to cry to God out of the depths.

"Out of the Depths I Cry Unto Thee"

I recall my fiftieth birthday as a good landmark. I liked to tell my younger women friends that forty is the pits, but fifty is wonderful.

A major ingredient in this happiness was that I had broken away from my teaching post at Loyola Marymount and was now a philosophy professor at the Archdiocesan Seminary of Los Angeles, under the chairmanship of Dr. Patrick Mitchell — he and his family being dear old friends. The change in job required a major decision away from financial security to a situation of little guarantee of a job but with much more fulfillment.

I was able to think of such a change because the combination of Martin's social security, interest on money saved and on the sale of our large family dwelling made it possible to consider dropping the portion of support coming from my fixed salary to half what it had been.

For years I had been furious that I had to work at a job I had come to find extremely unsatisfying in order to provide for the family items I considered to be more luxuries than necessities. That anger went no place except to embitter my heart and make my husband defensive.

When, finally, with the approval of my spiritual director I was ready to insist on taking a position with a lower salary, I didn't fret and fume. Instead, with fear and trembling indeed, but with complete conviction, I announced that I was planning to leave my tenured position as Full Professor to spend my time in a combination of part-time teaching at the Seminary, workshops and lectures.

For two days, my warm, loving husband turned cold with fury. Unwilling to witness this scene, my daughter Carla invited us both out for pizza. We sat at opposite ends of the table, pretending nothing was wrong. Finally, Martin cut off a piece of pizza and extended it to me with this funny remark: "Well, we vow to be together for better or worse. It's too bad that my wife is an idiot, but I guess I have to accept it." Making so bold and important a decision for myself, taking away a major daily cause of resentment, led to a happy release of love for Martin.

I also loved most everything about teaching at the Seminary. Here were older men taking their required philosophy classes. Heading toward ordination in the Catholic priesthood, they liked my way of mingling academic philosophy with defense of the faith, psychology and spirituality. Always dreaming of being part of a Catholic community, here I was teaching, eating, and going to Mass and prayer with a group I regarded as the heroes of our troubled times. After all, how many men can respond to a vocation that demands that much sacrifice in a time of so much hedonism? I loved to ponder Christ's choice of these men who will be spiritual warriors in the Church of the future.

One of the difficult parts was that I had still not overcome my co-dependency pattern. This had two sides. There were some men I would attach myself to for dear life who were exceedingly warm people, eager to give me the warmth and understanding I needed. These were few and far between: men like Dr. Frank Sullivan of Loyola Marymount, who was everybody's best friend, or Charles Rich, who is not only loving but also holy. In spite of anxiety attacks about losing them, these friendships were fundamentally good and graced.

The other track consisted of latching onto another type, men who have bottled-up deep sweetness and tenderness inside. They have psychological reasons why they cannot overflow in love to anyone, or not to a woman. The result of trying to be close to such men was that I found myself giving them vast quantities of attention and getting back a small amount. This left me feeling rejected and miserable.

Meanwhile, my daughter Carla married a wonderful young man, Peter Conley. Although I was sad that they were not married in the Catholic Church, I couldn't help seeing Peter as a gift from God. A successful engineering scientist with a fine income, he is intelligent, loving, kind, and devoted to helping Carla and their children in a lifestyle that involves, I would guess, some six hours a day of

"Out of the Depths I Cry Unto Thee"

attention to small details of family life. Since we now live together in an extended family house (Martin, myself, Carla, Peter, and their children Nicholas and Alexander) I can enjoy firsthand the happy results of my son-in-law's good character which complements my daughter Carla's emphatic, loving heart and creative ways of writing, decorating, and cooking.

Carla and Peter Conley

Now I want to return to the early part of the dreadful years of 1987-1993 when my main prayer consisted in groaning in the spirit, numb repetition of the rosary, and crying out of the depths to a God I knew was real but who seemed more distant than during the time of contemplative prayer I wrote of in the last chapter.

The terrible times began with my mother's dying process. Some of this I have described in the first chapter about the final reconciliation of my mother and myself as she lay on a special hospital bed in our house in her eighty-eighth year. Having her so close was a hard choice. Ultra-critical, she liked to goad me about everything in my character she found disagreeable. Besides, working full-time, commuting one and a half hours each way to the Seminary, and coming home to housework, it seemed just too much to add having my sick mother with us, even though she had saved so much money over her lifetime that she could easily afford an attendant.

During the year 1986, we had watched her condition deteriorate mentally as well as physically so that she had to move out of her partial-care, luxurious, ocean-view residence in Santa Monica to a small facility with locked doors for much more disabled people. Handling these matters with her had become a major cross, especially since she still regarded me as the "bad" daughter and my twin Carla as the "good" daughter. I resented suggestions my sister would make by long distance telephone from New York City. If she wanted to remain the "good daughter" why didn't she take over?

In spite of some very tense moments during visits of my sister to Los Angeles, she was the best at bringing my mother to accept reasonable changes. In her gentle, grace-filled way, rather than trying to force my somewhat senile mother to do something necessary, Carla would find images of why it might be better to move from a free place to a more secure one that would work on my mother's imagination rather than setting up a debate.

By this time my mother was in a wheelchair and my little granddaughter, also living with Diana at our house, was in a stroller. The two sometimes bumped up against each other and neither could disentangle the wheels. At one of these moments, I asked my mother whether she enjoyed having a great granddaughter. She replied: "Of course. We have a lot in common. We're both bored to death living here!"

Given my schedule, I did very little in terms of spending time with her. I was able to arrange for Fr. Grady, our parish priest, to come and give her the Anointing of the Sick. It was comforting to know that in the end she was receiving sacraments after a hiatus where she went to Church only occasionally. At the Residence near the ocean, I used to bring her holy communion. She responded by laughing at me! "See, Ronda, you say there will never be women priests. What a contradiction. Now you are one!"

I had been trying to get my mother into one of the beautiful Catholic nursing homes in the area but that did not work out. There was too long a waiting list. Calling a non-religious agency to send a twenty-four hour home aide, we first had a few unsuitable women. Finally, they sent a Filipino woman named Felicitas. This wonderful, holy woman had worked for a while as a lay helper for the Missionaries of Charity in the Philippines. Her idea of nursing was to spend the whole day praying the rosary and getting the patient to sing charming, charismatic songs "Now we're going to go to the Father's house where there's joy, joy, joy." It brings tears to my eyes to think that at that eleventh hour my sophisticated rationalistic mother was brought to spiritual childhood.

"Out of the Depths I Cry Unto Thee"

A large part of the psychological burden when my mother moved into a room in our house was assumed by Martin, who overcame his resentment of her years of hate toward him, reaching out to her with companionable love and holding her when she was shaking with fear in the night. A poem I wrote at the time expressed my sense of the last stage of her journey:

> *Tired from the long journey upstream*
> *Her soul reads water;*
> *scans the dark night*
> *for what is to come.*
>
> *We who would be lighthouses*
> *seem but flickering vigil candles*
> *on the remote shore.*
>
> *Into Thy hands we commend her spirit.*
>
> *Our Lady, Star of the Sea,*
> *guide her home.*

The last day of her life, the doctor recommended that she go into a nursing home again. I think he wanted to stop the pattern of having her on the verge of death and having us call the paramedics for resuscitation when he knew she was dwindling away and could not recover. After her death, we were told that she just stopped breathing.

The funeral was beautiful. We arranged to have a Mass said by one my mother's favorite Jesuit priests. Carla did a sacred dance to music of Howells that Martin had picked out. Since my mother had refused to decide whether she wanted to be buried or cremated, I gave into Carla's wish to have her cremated, and we had some of the ashes scattered in the ocean and some buried at a monastery cemetery.

In a subtle bonding between Carla and myself, when we got our $30,000 or so from the inheritance, we went to a thrift shop, as we had in childhood so often, to buy a suit and a dress. The rest we each gave to our husbands.

In the year 1990, feeling unusually exhausted, I sought the advice of Dr. Harvey Schneir, the husband of one of my closest friends, Cathy, also a Jew who became a Catholic. I had a complete physical examination. To my shock, the mammogram revealed breast cancer!

Not much of a lover of life, my initial reaction was to praise God that I now had a swift way to get away from this cross-filled earth. Naturally my spiritual director agreed with Martin that surgery and chemotherapy could not be considered an unnecessary extraordinary means for a woman of fifty-three. For hours, Martin tenderly worked on me to convince me that he would see me through the pain and love me even with one breast less.

Once I decided I would undertake the drastic treatments, God gave me the grace to focus on funny elements about my cancer. I started announcing around the seminary that it was okay to lose a breast because "less is more," or, with the faculty, to joke: "You always say that I am too one-sided, now God is proving it!"

Just before the surgery, I was giving a workshop that took place at Mount Angel near Portland, Oregon. Sitting in the chapel to pray before the talk, I suddenly noticed a wounded side of Jesus on a large crucifix. I was inspired to realize that after breast surgery my side would look like the chest of my Savior. A sort of natural stigmata!

This twin-image brought me through the surgery and the sad moment of looking at my unbalanced "new look" for the first time in the mirror. Nothing could reconcile me to the chemotherapy which I went through with great sighs and groans. So far, it looks as if they caught the cancer successfully. Praise the Lord.

I now venture into the worst part of this story. We left my son Charlie graduating in a blaze of glory from Hamilton High. Offered scholarship at several Universities, he chose UCLA because he liked the atmosphere there. I wanted him to go to some small Catholic university such as Franciscan University of Steubenville or Ignatius Institute within the University of San Francisco. He thought such schools would turn out to be too homogenous. He wanted to go someplace where he could explore with-

"Out of the Depths I Cry Unto Thee"

out constraints of having to fit in with some conformist mentality the whole student body was expected to be part of.

Shortly after classes began at UCLA, with Charlie living at home with us in a condo in Venice nearby, we noticed that he was depressed. The composition teacher at UCLA seemed to be involved in music much more contemporary and shorter in length, than the kind Charlie wrote, with long beautiful melodies and a Shostakovich kind of melancholy. Charlie was more or less given to understand that his work to date was high school stuff and that he must start fresh to learn composition in a set way they had designed.

Charlie, age 1-1/2

Experimenting with odd clothing resembling that of street people set him apart from the more conventional students. He missed his old girlfriend whom he had broken up with because he thought she couldn't truly understand the quest he was on. Soon he became unhappy enough to seek out counseling at the UCLA center. The psychologist there seemed in agreement with one he had seen for awhile in high school. He needed to find outlets for his anger. He had been too much the good, gifted child who pleased by going along with the heavy projections of family members.

In spite of his depression, he got grades in the B plus range for the first semester. Although everyone in the family but me knew he had lost his virginity, he still went to Mass on Sundays with us and spent lots of time in prayer. It seemed the knowledge that his Chinese girlfriend from High School would have an abortion if she got pregnant was one of the reasons he left her. He had

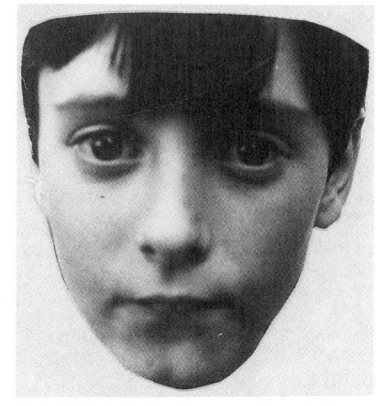

Charlie, age 12

once gotten drunk to the point of passing out when a friend introduced him to whiskey at Disneyland, but we heard nothing about drugs. In fact, he told us that he was instrumental in getting some of his friends off drugs.

During the interim, Charlie and his close friends from High School decided to shave their heads. Not having told us about it, he took off alone for a trip to the snow of Northern California. To convince Martin that this was a good idea he had to be strong and insistent. Even though we were worried about accidents, we finally agreed, thinking he needed some solitude. From far away, he told us about the shaven head. So lightly did we take these events as symptomatic of what most teenagers go through that we arranged a clownish home-coming for him. Knowing he adored the idea of the Double in Dostoevsky's novel about an insane man who imagines that his double has taken his place at work and is persecuting him, my daughters whose faces were almost identical to Charlie's dressed up in his clothing with hats on their heads to make it look as if they were his doubles and also had shaved heads. When he came in the door, he laughed and laughed at this prank. Later he claimed he didn't think it funny at all.

The long trip away from the family seemed to have done him some good. Back at UCLA, hair grown in thickly again, he started off on a new venture. His purpose would not be to succeed in the music department but rather to experiment with trying to be himself in a spontaneous manner, throwing off the fears that made him afraid not to conform. Since the activities he initiated seemed wild but delightful, we were not alarmed. After all, our daughters had dropped out of High School and gone in for life-styles much more frightening.

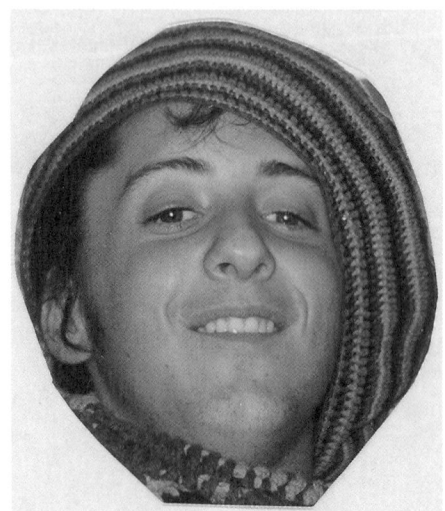

Charlie at college

Apparently there is an outdoor theater at UCLA, rarely

used during the day. Charlie liked to mount the stage and orate in a kind of manic clownish manner. He said people came around and enjoyed it. We had often thought Charlie should be an actor, for he was incredibly good at impersonation. In a thrilling move, he asked the head of an organization on campus that ran soapbox talks during lunch hour if he could give a pro-life speech. They had never known any student to want to do such a thing and agreed immediately for the sake of variety. How proud I was when he came home and I realized he had the guts to make an impassioned presentation of the wonder of new life at that anti-life University without even collecting any allies to back him up.

During the first summer, I wanted him to get a job. I had always thought this would be a good idea. Having taught at the University for seventeen years, I was familiar with the type of uncertainty about majors so many students go through. Sometimes working at some routine task for a low salary helps focus the student on what he might prefer to earn money at in the future. But since he wanted so much to spend the summer on composition and we knew he was capable of devoting himself to long hours in this fine pursuit, we were happy to see him busy working on a quartet and a beautiful piece for six strings called *Requiem for a Lost Childhood*.

To my joy, Charlie was becoming more religious. At Church, he liked to sit alone crouched in the back meditating. He went off in his pickup truck, useful for toting his large cello around, to the desert in the middle of the summer. He vowed to sit in the blazing sun until God spoke to him. After three hours of intense waiting, he did hear God speak to him clearly in his heart. God said that people don't believe in Him because they don't want to. They want total control of their own lives. At this point, Charlie reported that he surrendered to God.

The first indication of a crisis came on a Saturday morning in December just after we had moved into our extended family house in Woodland Hills with Carla, Peter, and their one year old baby Nicholas. Charlie called me into his room. He was shaking. He told me he had planned to jump off a huge rock in Topanga Canyon State Park called Eagle Rock. He had put suicide letters in the mailboxes of his friends, but then, at the last moment, had decided not to go through with it.

Terrified, we sent him immediately to the psychologists he had known and seemed to like from high school days. This time he resisted therapy. By Christmas vacation, the main thing we noticed is how much sleep he needed. He also stopped seeing his friends or even talking to them on the phone. We thought he was ashamed of his suicide attempt and wanted to renew himself before resuming these intense relationships with young men and women who saw him as their leader.

His final day at UCLA we now see as tragically symbolic. He had joined an improvisation class. They had a concert at the end of the quarter featuring the compositions of the students. Most of these were short cacophonous pieces in the contemporary mode. Charlie prefaced the playing of his lyrical *Requiem for the Lost Childhood* with a short speech telling about his feelings about the wonder of youth. No one responded either to the poetic speech or to the composition with anything but politeness. Charlie saw this lack of response as a sign of the hopelessness of ever succeeding in the music scene of our times.

New Year's Day, January 1, 1991, we had a large family gathering. Charlie had grown to hate big holiday dinners. He wanted to take off, but we were a little apprehensive. Instead, we pretended he was sick and brought food to his room all day. At about 5 P.M., he was going stir crazy and we let him go out with the recycle cans to the local depository.

When by 7 P.M. he had not come back, my husband began to get extremely tense. We starting driving around the neighborhood in the dark looking for his truck. Passing our own mailbox we noticed it was open — odd for the evening. In the box was a ripped off piece of paper with the words "Eagle Rock" in Charlie's handwriting.

While my son-in-law called the police, we took off for Topanga State Park, convinced that the words Eagle Rock were his way of telling us that this time he would jump. The park was closed. I had once gone hiking with Charlie to Eagle Rock so I thought I might be able to get to the top in time to dissuade him in case he was sitting there undecided, as we all have seen on TV news or in the movies.

My husband considers that this night was the worst in his life. Asthmatics avoid going out in the night air. They never go on hikes.

"Out of the Depths I Cry Unto Thee"

Nobody goes out to deserted State Parks at night in the Los Angeles area. So both of us were risking our lives to try to save our son. And in spite of the terrible fear, we felt an unusual closeness. In our everyday life, it was rare for each of us to experience the same emotions at the same time. Along the narrow trail we went, totally lost, the moon shining brightly, with the sound of coyotes howling in the distance, crying out his name between wracking sobs.

Finally, we passed the Ranger Station. They had heard from the police that we were coming. A ranger was out looking for Charlie. I called home to tell Carla that we, at least, were safe. She yelled: "Charlie is on the other phone!"

He said he was at the pay phone in the parking lot. It was just a few yards from the Station. We rushed out to grab him and hug him. He was trembling and crying and saying that he couldn't do it, and now he knew it was the wrong path. "You should lock me up, I'm really crazy."

The police had not yet come. The Ranger made a report and told us to take him to UCLA Emergency. To our surprise, the psychiatrist there did not insist on locking him up. She said to take him home and watch him, and seek out a psychiatrist the next day. The doctor we met with next day told us that he thought Charlie was a manic-depressive with symptoms typical of creative people. He listed names of famous men who had committed suicide. He suggested that Charlie should agree himself to go to an institute at UCLA where they study the effect of certain medicines on moods. If he did not wish to go, he thought we should insist, if necessary with the help of police force.

Charlie refused to go. Scenes of "One Flew Over the Cuckoo's Nest" came readily to mind and he told us he would never go to such a place. At first we were inclined to force him to go, but when we got home he seemed very positive. He said he would never do it again, and we should just let him drop out of UCLA, rest for a quarter and find out what he wanted to do without any pressure. Meanwhile he would be under constant surveillance, quite possible with a household of four adults around him. I was home for semester break from the seminary.

Charlie spent his time sleeping, eating huge quantities of food, putting all his music onto the computer, and playing with his little nephew. For the next six weeks, Carla gave him a salary for watching the baby while she did her home computer work. It was a joy to see Charlie setting off around the block with his large walking stick, our huge Great Pyrennees dog and the baby, singing, telling stories, and collecting leaves. He seemed like some sort of cross between Zarathustra and St. Francis.

During these six weeks, he also spent about three hours a day talking to Martin. Always very close, the two were drawn together even more as my life-loving husband tried to encompass with his empathy and wisdom the type of despair that could lead his brilliant, beloved son to so low an ebb.

At the end of his six weeks at home, Charlie started talking about going back to UCLA to take literature, a subject he knew he could do well in without the slightest pressure. My husband continually assured him that even if he never did anything we would take care of him. Charlie seemed to drink in this unconditional love and to be ready to make his own choices. He swore he would never try suicide again.

Diana and Pete Jump

He became incredibly loving to the family during these days. He would spend hours with his sister Diana and her little girl Jenny. Diana had just gotten married to Pete Jump, a large handsome man, originally from the South with a wonderful smile and sparkling eyes and, as a bonus, some Native American blood. I like the strength of mind and will he manifests. Pete works on computer training programs at the same company where Diana was doing telephone sales contacts. He plays baseball on the side. We were happy to see Diana settled at last.

"Out of the Depths I Cry Unto Thee"

Charlie got me to go on bike rides with him, laughing and joking so I would be sure he was safe. His last deep word to me was this: "Mom, I know you think you are a terrible Christian because of your great limits (especially bad temper). You are limited. But I think you are a wonderful Christian because ... you have no defenses!"

Then he began to plead for a short vacation before returning to UCLA. He reminded us of the trip to the snow that had done him so much good the year before. My husband was frightened. Suppose he got suddenly depressed again? Go with a friend. But his friends were not available. We happened to remember a beautiful monastery in the mountains of Big Sur overlooking the Pacific: The Immaculate Heart Hermitage, a branch of the Camaldolese monks of whom it was Padre Benedetto in Italy who had married us.

It seemed like a good idea. The monks could keep an eye on him. He would be surrounded by beauty. He would not have to talk to anyone because the hermits try to be silent most of the time. He was to call us every day for sure and come back after a week. He was to start home on Thursday.

On Thursday, February 21, we received this letter in the mail:

Dear Family,
I have discovered that the fathomless currents of my soul which once overflowed within me to give me new life have now flowed past the green valleys and mountains, which are purpose and hope, and have reached the sea, which is death. The very force within me which hitherto brought me rebirth and a glorious bubble of dreams, now turns backwards toward destruction since the vanquishment of all that gave joy and savor to life. When I see the incredible beauty of waterfalls, rivers, forests, and oceans my spirit knows that the life force is long gone and that the roads I once traveled by can never be walked again, and hope was a bittersweet dream of the past, and the only pure, beautiful road that nature opens is a fall toward my friend, the end.

Father, you must understand you are in no way to blame for the course of events. If it were not for the fact that I have slipped beyond the salvation of humanity, your efforts would have done miraculous wonders to help me. My life is your life and yours is mine and many a time have we given each other light in the darkness. Yet how could you possibly help me when I have known, yet, I know

En Route To Eternity

beyond doubt that my cycle is over and all I can do is walk towards the darkness, which is the end. I know this so deeply that none can save me. Better that I am free to pursue my destiny with beauty and integrity than that another man or institution pretends to protect me from what will always be so. I have searched all my life and found "nothing" on the top of Mt. Carmel. It is as true and natural as the dust from which we came.

God has been good to me, for I have found the most beautiful country in all the world on which to lay my head. Just north of Andrew Molera State Park and Point Sur there is an enormous arched bridge. A rainbow bridge which spans a quiet valley in which there lies a green meadow covered with yellow flowers surrounding a river which runs through the birch trees then curves to make its way through a land of green ivy then swirls through the sand to make a final passage to the sea. I will land in the green meadow then perhaps be carried to the ocean if I am lucky. I can image no more beautiful and perfect way to witness the end of time.

These finals days spent in nature and at the monastery have purified my soul and given me peace for my departure. Considering myself, I realize that it is right that I should die as a child still within sight of my youth and all of the wonders and treasures, and creations, and laughter, and songs which make up Charlie, yet will be no more. I am not sad that I never became a man because if I look even fleetingly at the possibility of the future I feel only dread and loathing. I am the King of the Past. In my kingdom I have experienced all the love and fulfillment and colors and dimensions that a person can hope for. I see no cause for grief. As a free spirit, wanderer and pilot of my destiny I cry to all you that I love.

FAREWELL, Charlie Chervin

Soon after Martin read this letter, Charlie called on the phone. "Hello. I'm filling the car up with gas. On my way."

My husband was stunned. When he told Charlie that he had gotten the suicide letter, Charlie said "Oh, no!" as casually as if it were a broken social engagement. In a state of terrible fear, my husband begged him to go back to the monastery and wait for him to arrive. He agreed. Martin said we would not call the police if he waited for us. But we had to call the police. They say they planted one squad car at the monastery and one at the bridge he described in his note. They told us to stay home in case he was headed home.

"Out of the Depths I Cry Unto Thee"

I couldn't stand it. I left Martin home with the family and decided I would fly up to San Jose, the nearest airport to Big Sur and then drive Charlie home in the truck when the police located him.

"Out of the depths I cry to Thee" (Psalm 130). All the way I prayed incessantly, mostly cries of Jesus, Jesus, Jesus, or Hail Mary's over and over again. And yet I still really thought he was bluffing. I am sure you have heard the theory that those who leave notes around to let you know "before" are really just crying out for help.

My sister's husband, Arthur, came from Berkeley where they now live near the Pacific School of Religion, to meet me at the airport and drive me down to Big Sur. I don't think it was until I was enfolded in his tight hug on arrival that I remembered that his son by a former marriage had committed suicide as a young adult by jumping off a building in New York City.

The ride took a very long time. On the way we stopped at phone booths where I called home to see if the police had called with good news. It was foggy and the roads were windy. About an hour away from the monastery, now traveling in darkness, we stopped at a motel with a bar to make another call. They told us that the monastery gates closed at 9 P.M. and we should stay overnight at the motel. Frustrated I decided to put in a call to the local police before retiring.

> *"Hello, this is Mrs. Chervin, the one whose son Charles you are looking for, did you find him yet?"*

> *"Wait a minute, give us your number and the detective will call you back."*

Rock music banging away from the bar, I waited for the call.

> *"Are you Mrs. Chervin?"*

> *"Yes."*

> *"Oh that one! He jumped. He's dead! Do you mind if I ask you a few questions?"*

By that time, Arthur had grabbed hold of me. I let out a shriek but then decided I should call Martin rather than have him hear the same terrible words in the cold voice of a stranger.

It happened that the paramedic who had gone down the mountain on ropes to get Charlie was at the bar drinking. He asked if I would be willing to let him talk to me. He does this as volunteer work. A burly tough guy, he told me he had been summoned just minutes after the jump. A hitchhiker had seen him standing by the concrete railing of the bridge — it was a smaller one (but 170 feet down) than that mentioned in his letter, which was why the police were not there. Then he went back to the truck, grabbed a blanket, and leaped. The paramedic said that his body was intact. His heart would have given out from the pressure of the fall. He landed on his feet. And Charlie's face had a peaceful look when they found him.

Did Jesus catch him on the way down? At home my husband noticed that the clock had stopped at 4 P.M. the moment Charlie jumped. He heard an audible voice, Charlie's voice, say "Dad, I'm okay."

Reluctantly, the police said I could see Charlie's body in the mortuary the next morning if I came early enough. Arthur bought a bottle of wine and let this potion give me the freedom to let out all my screaming misery held tight in his embrace. Needless to say, the intense sympathetic love Arthur showed me at this most dreadful time created a bond that no amount of disagreement about anything can ever sever.

Carla, my twin, arrived next morning. She loved Charlie very much and identified with him as someone in the arts like herself. Carla went in with me to the room where we could see his head at the top of the body bag. All through the night I had been identifying this last encounter on earth with the Pieta. Like Mary, I was going to hold my dead son in my arms, and Mary would be there to help me through it.

Charlie looked beautiful! Nothing like embalmed corpses. His face looked solemn and focused. I had fantasies of Christ resurrecting him like Lazarus. I kissed his cool forehead and his heavy wet brown hair and prayed while laying relics of St. Catherine of Siena and Conchita on his head. My sister laid the cross she had received at baptism on him, and did a slow dance around his body. I kissed him one last time saying "Good-bye, sweet prince."

I asked for a clump of his hair which I sewed into a piece of the kimono my mother wore when giving birth to us. This tight little ball of Charlie I wore next to my heart for almost a year.

Originally I thought the whole family would drive up from Los Angeles and we would have a funeral Mass in Monterey. Martin was too prostrate with grief to go anywhere. He sat in his chair for a night and a day weeping inconsolably. He thought Charlie's body should be cremated and scattered in the ocean as his final letter expressed such a desire to be in the ocean.

On the trip to the monastery where I donated Charlie's pickup truck, my sister Carla held on to me and prayed the rosary with me. I will never forget the maternal sweetness of my twin on that day. Arthur mentioned that right after we heard about Charlie's death he smelled roses all around the grounds of the motel, though there were no roses. Arthur is not a Catholic. He had never heard of St. Therese of Lisieux's promise to send roses from heaven. But I knew and felt comforted.

Finally they left me at San Jose airport for my trip home to all those waiting in even greater misery than I for not having said good-bye.

Never, never, never, had we known such grief. For days and nights Martin and I lay on our bed sobbing and blaming ourselves as we went back over what seemed like every moment of Charlie's life trying to understand. Later, during helpful crisis therapy with a suicide expert I would come to see that parents can never come to clear conclusions about why their child killed himself or herself. The same factors exist in so many lives and don't lead to suicide.

All kinds of suggestions were made. It came from a chemical imbalance. Nothing would have helped. These and these remedies would have helped. The explanation that helped us the most because it fit Charlie's character was advanced by the psychologist Joseph Nicolosi about the eternal child syndrome. Typically, the crisis comes when the ego dies, overwhelmed by the task of making the transition to an adulthood that is fiercely rejected. It was reassuring to learn that such eternal children generally do not respond to therapy so the terrible thought that if we had locked him up he would have been saved was improbable.

From the moment of Charlie's death, the miracles started to flow. My sister Carla heard Charlie say, "I love my sisters. Father, forgive me and hold my hand. But mother, you taught me not to fear death." She had an image of Charlie stroking my hair and laughing. Within the next few days in Woodland Hills, visitors came in and would stroke my hair as if Charlie's hand was moving them.

Friends of mine with mystical gifts began to see Charlie in the light, saved, full of peace and strength. Sister Mary Neill came and slept in his bed. She started to sob in the night over his tragic end. She heard him say, "Sing no sad songs for me." Some seminarians who had never met Charlie felt his presence or special graces coming to them through his intercession. Little Jenny felt his presence and he told Diana's husband Pete that he was okay and that Pete should strengthen the family. In a longer book I wrote about Charlie, I have some 100 signs of this sort to report.

For me the greatest comfort came when I went to the monastery where I am an Oblate, St. Andrew's Priory. Having run myself ragged with details of funeral Masses, being in the chapel was the first time I sat perfectly still. I heard Jesus tell me in my heart very clearly and strongly: "I let him jump because I could not stand to watch him suffer so much. The purpose of life is to get a foretaste of heaven and to want eternity. That is what he wanted. He had his foretastes of eternity in the joys of life. He was weaned by his sufferings from wanting to live any more. You will find him in My heart."

Talking afterwards to Fr. Gregory Elmer, who had been Charlie's godfather, I seemed to see Charlie in Gregory's eyes just as one can see Juan Diego in the eyes of Our Lady of Guadalupe when her face imprinted on the mantle of Juan is enlarged by modern photographic techniques.

No matter how many signs we have that Charlie is saved, we would never conclude that his act could have been right or good. It was a tragic, violent move. Reading the journals that he wrote the last year and left at the monastery, it is clear that he was deeply troubled in his mind and soul. God knows all hearts. We believe that he is forgiven. The last words in the journal are, "Save Me! Save Me! Save Me!"

"Out of the Depths I Cry Unto Thee"

That cry from the depths has become my prayer. For the last two and a half years since Charlie's death, my only hope lies in the Mercy of Jesus. The famous mercy prayer of Blessed Faustina I previously thought mawkish now is my only solace when I sink into grief.

The support I received from friends was incredibly soothing. I want to tell any of you who read this autobiography how grateful I still am for everything you did.

There are four close friends who stood by me in ways that need special mention. Cathy Schneir, a woman of deep spirituality and also of delicate perceptiveness, knew how to open me up to talk about the most horrible of my feelings during the worst days.

Richard Geraghty, a colleague at St. John's, a wonderful warm, pungent, funny, and profound person, sustained me at work by letting me run on and on over lunch. His friendship was particularly healing because he got engaged to be married shortly after Charlie's death. With my pattern of fear of abandonment, the announcement of his engagement triggered off my father complex. Surely bonded to this new and younger woman, he would have no time for me who was only, after all, a friend. The sensitive manner in which he managed to persuade me of my place in his life even though I was in pieces over Charlie most of the times we met had the effect of finally healing this troubled part of my psyche.

Patricia Treece was the third friend to stand with me under the cross holding me up. A true intercessor, this writer of books about the saints, helped me to get the grace to understand that my dark feelings of despair were classical. With soft persuasive words she convinced me of my need for rest, good food, relaxation.

Of course my great spiritual friend, Charles Rich, who was convinced that his namesake was saved, and who still showers me with letters about the reality of eternity, was an abiding source of light and hope.

As a result of so much pain I find that in my talks I have more ready access to the heart's of my listeners than ever before. I have earned my credentials as a sufferer. My words no longer have any ring of the clichés that come to the lips of those not touched by so deep a grief.

A year ago, I became a lay handmaid of the Sacred Heart of Jesus, Mary and Joseph, for that image of the merciful Heart is so dear to me. I had an interior vision this year of my heart linked to that of Jesus with a heavy knot made up of the mutual cords. Jesus seemed to tell me, I have wed you in pain. Your name is Ronda of the Precious Blood.

I do not want to seem to be so grateful for the special graces that were given to console us concerning our son's death that a despairing reader might take it into his or her head that suicide is a good way to skip over life and leap into eternity. Every day grief pierces our hearts. If only he had agreed to go to a Catholic psychotherapist or spiritual director who might have helped him find a way whether medical or other to be freed from the intensity of his interior pain. If only he could have found his way to embrace Jesus as his Saviour on earth so that he could have served Him, yes, in fear and trembling, carrying the cross, but also rejoicing in the good things in life that are God's gifts to us. I pray that each reader who is suicidal who reads this may try everything possible to avoid so terrible a death.

And Martin? Who besides me was there for Martin at this worst time of his life? First of all our daughters. Carla and Diana have gone to great lengths to manifest their love for Martin so that he should not feel his fatherhood was void. They both conceived little baby boys right after the tragedy, and these sweet cute rollicking grandsons have joined Jenny and Nicholas to lighten his spirits.

Martin's closest friend, Gabriel Meyer, came over that awful night and sat up with him. He was willing to figure out the piano score for Charlie's *Requiem for a Lost Childhood* and play it at the memorial Mass. A man in his forties, Gabriel is a little too mature and independent to fit in completely as a substitute son, but he does serve this role partly by visiting us frequently and showing his love for the whole family in so many endearing ways.

God himself seemed to be comforting Martin through new successes with his plays. Dan Ferrone, and actor and director, who came over to pray the rosary for Charlie as an act of compassion, was able to produce a video version of *Born/Unborn*. Pamela Fields, an actress living in Phoenix is putting on *Myself: Alma Mahler*. Since Martin had resigned himself about production and used to tell

"Out of the Depths I Cry Unto Thee"

Charlie that someday he would take over his father's work to bring it to the public, I certainly think it is Charlie from eternity who has arranged these successes.

Like most introverts, Martin has mostly had to work out his feelings within his own heart. Four months after the death he wrote this prose-poem for Charlie:

Charlie, My Charlie,
Did you think you could leave me so easily
and I wouldn't follow my gazelle
loping through magic redwoods
to live in a peaceful Hobbit village
under a Bridge of Rainbows?
Yes,
I heard the threatening hoofs,
Black Riders behind you.
Yes.
I heard the music pause ... stop.
Each note wrenched out in torment
emptied itself in silence.

You know I was watching
when the dark world descended full force,
trying to urge your soul from your body.
I looked into your mirror
as the fuzz touched your cheek
and the knowing look replaced
the innocent sparkle.

But you fought the good, clean battle for which
in good faith
you will be forgiven ... and I
fought with you.

You wanted to be me
and I was you.
Would that I had died instead
of you!
Would that you had inherited
my life force!
But maybe you did,
finding your better strength
in the knowledge that
to survive such a world

En Route To Eternity

*is a defeat
of the spirit.*

*Time is not yet
the healer.
I mourn with those of our bone and blood
left behind,
feeling your absence.
With your mother who bore you
in hope and prayer
between the trials of miscarriage.
With Carla and Diana
your other selves,
with those new lives
whose hearts sprang with joy
whenever you entered the door
and spoke their language.*

*You must know that I take the sacrament
in the name of The Charlie —
that cocky, free, creative spirit
leaning on Fanghorn,
his magic wand,
observing the world through the eyes
of the Eternal Child:
alive in the morning that never ends.*

*This, in the spirit of Christ,
who descended the cross
to revive hope in the world!
It has taken the edge off
the sting of death
that someday
we will be attending
each other.
I pray that those of my family
who arrived ahead of me
will embrace you in love
and remind You of us,
waiting.*

*You know that I would have done
everything in my power
to postpone your exit.
But after that leap into tragedy,
I know too well, after the fact,*

"Out of the Depths I Cry Unto Thee"

*that we could not have endured
the assaults on The Charlie Spirit
that would have made a mockery of your innocent dreams,
flaying your body to get at
your precious source.*

*You protected us from that —
and I must say
through my tears —
for that much,
I am grateful.
You spared us the torture
of watching you suffer,
forcing us to compromise
with the unnatural.*

*Still, had we the power of choice —
20 years of your lovable being
ending in a constant sense of loss,
or not knowing you at all —
how gladly would we
pay the fee,
with what tremulous joy!*

*Permit me to mourn
the reversal of nature,
father burying son,
while I keep my faith.
By sending this letter,
you know my yearning.
I miss
your handsome face,
gentle big eyes:
intelligent,
looking to learn the light,
hopeful for secrets.*

*I keep looking for you
impatiently
in the fullness of memory.
I cannot wait.
Our lives were so entwined,
flesh works havoc on my spirit
as I remember your beautiful music,
striking the keynote,
the essences of our lives*

En Route To Eternity

*together on earth.
I am still tortured
by all the questions
you asked of your father,
thinking the power of healing was mine.
It wasn't!*

*We surrounded you
with art and beauty
and a deep respect for integrity.
Perhaps you would have been better served
if like me, the artful dodger,
we had taught you the crass arts of survival
while preserving your substance.
But then,
propped up by drugs and self-indulgence,
what would we have inherited
with the world as it is today?
A dead seed with no sunlight
to birth a flower.
Still...
you would be with us NOW!*

*I don't know!
We don't have such a choice!
I don't have any answers
except to repeat what your mother taught you:
He came down from the cross to save us!
Without that mysterious point in time to hold onto,
without the promise...
eternity —
what matters?
Is that why we were born?*

*I trust you have the answer, my son.
That it's not all silence, inspire us!
I pray it's so...*

*Take him, God!
He plays a decent cello.*[1]

---

[1] I have always loved the depth and poetic beauty of my husband's writing. If you are interested in finding about more about his pro-life play *Born/UnBorn* and *Myself, Alma Mahler*, about Alma and Gustav Mahler, or his masterpiece *Forty Days of Chiaro Oscuro*, about Christ and Satan in the desert, write to Carla Chervin Conley at 115 Yonder Lane, Sedona, AZ 86336 or call 1-800-437-2368. Same address to get a tape of Charlie's music.

Epilogue

Yesterday, I attended a play where I met an acquaintance of many years ago. "Are you pregnant?" she asked. "No, I'm just a fat old woman," I replied smiling.

This self-styled appellation pleased me. During chemotherapy, I found that only ice-cream shakes could get the horrible taste of medicines out of my mouth. The weight I gained at that time was augmented by the hormonal changes of menopause. At twenty-five, 5'4", I weighed 105 pounds. At thirty, 115. At forty, 125, and at fifty-six I weigh in at 140. Swaying as I waddle about in my large Mexican or Indian dresses, a throw-back to the pictures of gypsies and flamenco dancers my father loved, I feel like an earth grandmother, full of hard earned wisdom and grace.

The weeping over my son's death has slowly given way to resignation and shy hope. Eternity seems very close now. Those simple prayers of the unitive stage I mutter all day long are wafting me away from the world to the place where all tears will be dried.

During this time I have grown in my life as a Handmaid of the Sacred Heart of Jesus, Mary and Joseph.[1] Praying with the Handmaids and Servants led by Sister Mary Joseph and Fr. Luke

---

[1] For more information about the Handmaids, an order of Sister and lay prayer partners, write to: P. O. Box 2957, Ventura, CA 93002 or call (805) 653-2379 and about the Servants write to the Apostolate of Christian Renewal, 411 First Street, Fillmore, CA 93015, (805) 524-5890.

En Route To Eternity

Zimmer the Mystical Mass Prayer and Rosary my soul has become much more simple and detached. That is, much more attached to the Sacred Heart and less over-attached to relationships and projects. Since I find my loved ones best in the Sacred Heart I am less anxious to secure them by means of possessive and domineering ways of my own. Since I count on Christ more than myself to save the world I am less involved with the results of my own efforts as a teacher, speaker and writer.

Recently I met at the house of the Servants Barbara Matthais who believes she is receiving apparitions from Our Lady. Whatever may be the status of Church discernment about the matter, simply sitting next to her, I felt deep peace and also a sense of God drawing me deeply within where He dwells in my heart, with a sense of space between me and all earthly realities. This peace and detachment has lasted quite a while so that I am inclined to want to change the title of this epilogue from "A Fat Old Woman" to "A Fat Peaceful Old Woman."

After reading my autobiography, Fr. Luke Zimmer, told me he looks forward to the time when I will be more free in the spirit, living more out of the contemplative side of my nature. May it be so.

An outgrowth of this new phase of my life has been starting a Queen of Peace Center for Spiritual Formation with a deeply contemplative friend, Paul Griesgraber helping lead.

After finishing the first version of *En Route to Eternity,* my whole life changed. On October 9, 1993, my husband died suddenly of cardiac arrest.

Martin 1992

Epilogue

My daughter Carla and her family, with whom we were living, moved to Sedona, Arizona.

The earthquake came and with it also a chance to be a visiting professor at Franciscan University of Steubenville.

So, here I am suddenly a single pilgrim woman. Only nine months since Martin's death, I am too shaken to write of my feelings. Mostly, as Martin always wryly predicted, I miss him more than I thought I would. Without his earthiness, I am like a balloon in the sky. Without his fierce and domineering love I am like a lost silly soul. I cling to Christ and the Church and grab the hands of family and friends and wait for what God will send *en route to eternity*.

In the Appendix you will find the beautiful tributes my daughters read at Martin's funeral — literary gems in themselves. The splendidly arranged Mass was at St. Andrew's Abbey at Valyermo where we were both Oblates.

Eternity – God – Love – Unity – Me as We. I am certainly half-way to eternity, probably three-quarters of the way.

If you liked reading my story, will you pray that we will all meet up merrily in heaven? Glory be to the Father, the Son, and the Holy Spirit. Amen. Alleluia!

Appendix

Von Hildebrand's Refutations

Since some readers may themselves be unsure how to refute these pervasive mentalities, I will present here a brief summary of the refutations that can be found both in Von Hildebrand's books such as *What is Philosophy?* and *Ethics* and also in any text of Thomistic philosophy.

The skeptical point of view towards truth holds that there is absolutely no way for the human mind to arrive at any certainty about any important ideas. Nothing is true for all, there is only "truth for me."

By a refutation as old as Augustine in the third century, Von Hildebrand would show that skepticism was itself contradictory. Some truths must be held to be objective. "Even if I err, at least I know that the one who errs, myself, certainly exists to err," as St. Augustine put it. Von Hildebrand demonstrated this truth by writing on the blackboard the sentence to which all skeptics agree:

"There is no truth."

Look hard at that statement. Is it really true? If you say yes, then you are asserting that there is at least one truth, that sentence. But if there is even one truth this means the mind can grasp truth and then skepticism is false.

To a reader untrained in philosophy, such arguments may seem trivial indeed. But for those who have racked their brains about such questions for years, such refutations are crucial. Without the belief that truth can be found the whole enterprise of thought is undermined. Indeed the small number of philosophy students in non-religious Universities is mostly based on the fact that it is futile to study a subject which claims there is no truth to be found in its matter. Religious-based schools who know there is truth because God is truth attract much larger numbers of majors.

With respect to truth in the field of ethics what is needed to begin on solid ground is a refutation of relativism. Relativism is the theory that all our views of right and wrong are mere products of programming of a historical, social, biological or psychological nature.

According to relativists, when a person states "this is morally wrong," he or she is only revealing the results of programming in childhood. It is foolish to make pronouncements about what is absolutely good and evil if there is no way to transcend one's culture.

To this contemporary viewpoint, Von Hildebrand was totally opposed. He argued that basic moral truths are universal or should be so, even if there is a difference about some matters such as monogamy and polygamy, etc. Every person all over the world knows the difference between malice and kindness; between fidelity and betrayal. Every person has a sense of a moral ought which transcends his or her own immediate desires.

Even a person who claims that morality has no absolute validity in his own daily life will respond with moral indignation to the breadth of those rights he or she personally holds to be inalienable. To use a contemporary example, we don't hear women dismissing rape on the basis that there are no moral absolute, or Jewish people deciding that the Holocaust was a logical result of cultural forces in Germany and therefore was not absolutely wrong.

The differences that do exist from one society to the next, Von Hildebrand describes in his book *Ethics*. Whenever there are advantages to be gained by immoral practices, people will try to blind themselves to the evil and suffering involved. The practice of the slave trade in the United States provides a good example. In my own book called *Living in Love: About Christian Ethics* (St. Paul's Books and Media) I present a popularized proof of the objectivity of ethical norms especially with reference to such controversial issues as contraceptives, homosexuality, and issues concerning war and peace and social justice.

Appendix

My Thoughts on Several Issues

An Answer to Questions of Betrayal

My favorite response to the idea of some Jews that I have betrayed my people in becoming part of so evil a Church is to make a comparison with being a citizen of the United States in spite of the evils of racism that abound in our country. I am proud to be American because I think our Constitution sets forth true principles of government. The fact that we fail to live up to them in many ways doesn't convince me to leave our country but rather to seek ways to convince others to live up to these great founding ideas. Racism is anti-American and therefore not a reason not to be American. Persecution of the Jewish people is a slap in the face of Jesus, who was Jewish. Anti-Semitism is anti-Catholic and therefore not a reason not to be Catholic.

On Charismatic Renewal

A friend who recently joined a twelve-step group remarked that there was more community among the self-confessed addicts who met together out of need than in Catholic groups where people tend to show their best face.

I think this is true in the main, but it leaves out the tremendous grace it is for the Church to have a Catholic way, mostly, though not exclusively, found in charismatic renewal, to be with others where we can express any emotion freely and receive loving prayer on the spot. Not only do I benefit from being prayed over, but I love to pray myself over others. Instead of just saying, "I'm sorry you have that cross to bear, I will pray for you," how much more tender and direct is it to immediately hold the hurting person and pray God's healing love down upon him or her.

I suppose it is a matter of balance. I have come to realize that it is wrong to insist that everyone express themselves as freely as I feel comfortable doing. A priest once replied to my pleas for greater closeness in a group with the cold but true words: "Perhaps, Ronda, you need to earn our trust before demanding it!" With my childhood background of constant vehement Jewish-style dialogue, one of the hardest things to adjust to among most Catholics is that they insist on being private.

I have learned to see that this need, if not my own, is legitimate. After all Edith Stein, that transfigured holy Jewish convert, wrote about how much women especially need to learn how to let things develop in silence rather than to probe others in conversation out of curiosity.

My Books

How grateful I am to Liguori, the first publisher to want one of my writings: *Church of Love*. Ignatius Press, led by Fr. Joseph Fessio, whom I think of as a hero, had enough faith in my vision of how to combine the Feminine, the Free and the Faithful, to publish that book as well as others. Publishers such as Dove, Alba, and St. Bede's published some of the titles in spirituality. Daughters of St. Paul did their own reprints of former books as well as taking a chance on a book no one else seemed daring enough to publish: *Spiritual Friendship: the Darkness and the Light* which provides a road map of stages for readers confused about such deep but sometimes frightening bonds. Recently it has been Servant Books that has been most interested in commissioning me to write about the women saints and mystics. Chiaro Oscuro Press recently published my *Freed to Love: Healing for Catholic Women* for personal reflection, workshops, and retreats, a six session approach toward healing the mind, soul and spirit of women of faith.

Many of my books were written with co-authors so that I could be a "we" again. I wrote four books: *The Woman's Tale, Bringing the Mother With You, How Shall We Find The Father* (adding Don Briel) (Seabury Press), and *Great Saints, Great Friends* (Alba House) with Sister Mary Neill, a Dominican, whose insights and warmth have brightened my life for so many years. *Woman to Woman* (Ignatius Press) was written with Terri Vorndran Nichols, a former student.

Love of Wisdom (Ignatius Press) a large philosophy book came out of a collaboration with Msgr. Eugene Kevane during my time of teaching at Notre Dame Institute, Arlington, Virginia where Catholics can get M.A.'s in catechetics and spirituality studying summers or winters with fine professors loyal to the Magisterium.

Other co-authors I loved working with include Fr. Jim Maher with whom I wrote a fictional book of letters from a charismatic woman who "spiritually adopts" a late vocation seminarian. The book is called *Spiritual Friendship: A Contemporary Correspondence.* Lois Janis, a Jewish-ancestry member of the Unity Church helped me revise *Voyage to Insight,* and Msgr. Joseph Pollard and I collaborated on a book in defense of the Catholic Faith entitled *Tell Me Why: Answering Tough Questions About the Faith* (Our Sunday Visitor Press). I am presently working on a book with my daughter Carla on Catholic family traditions. Ross Porter and Gary Hapins are two recent co-authors.

Prayer Poems and Excerpts from Letters to Charles Rich

By day You breathe me out.
By night You breathe me in.
Will this rhythm never end?
And when it does will I be out or in?
Perfect Love Casteth Out Fear

An interior vision during the night – I saw us (Charlie Rich and myself) dancing with the saints and they were shouting:
"It is true, it is all true."
Glory be to the Father, the Son, and the Holy Spirit."

A Driver's Prayer

When I rode alone
along the path
of life
it was
Bang
Crash,
Totaled!

En Route To Eternity

*Now I ride with
Your right arm
around me
cushioned against
all shocks.*

*On my last excursion, Lord,
I will close my eyes
and let You
take me home.*

---

*Love in Heaven,
intense as lover's kiss,
soft as mother's breast,
freed as friend's delight,
caring as father's gaze,
secure as God's eternity.*

At Pecos monastery during the night, Jesus made me feel that it made no difference where I was or will be. I am in his heart. No more fantasies about ideal places to be, no more wishes, worries about the future.

Whenever I pray, the first thing Jesus says is that there is no reason for me to be so busy. He wants so much to give me His gift of peace. He wants me to be happy. The more active a nature, the more deeply it needs times of silence and deep openness to him. Sometimes I hear him saying over and over again to me "Your heart, your heart," because my brain races too fast over schemes for projects to convert the world while my heart gets more and more jumpy as a result of being left to be buffeted by every wind of life.

Sometimes I lie awake at night and feel all the pain of every soul I have met ... Martin had arisen in the night to write. The radio alarm tuned to music was playing Delius' cello concerto. Charlie (my son) came bounding in, beautiful and ruddy

Appendix

with enthusiasm. How glorious and radiant the world seemed ... but one little unpleasantness and off I was again – alas!

⁎⁎

Dancing now with You
rather than with
my thought of You
Suddenly I'm afraid

Like a middle-aged school teacher
a sailor might woo
gauche, shy, overcorsetted
in my fifty arguments
for Your truths

You swing me round and round
out on a limb

⁎⁎

I was walking on the boardwalk here, and at my first glance at the water, the words came to my mind that Jesus was saying "That is Me as water!" I gazed at it with great delight and then heard him telling me more: "See the beautiful seagull — that's Me as a seagull." Finally I heard him say, "See that Ronda, that's Me as Ronda!" It opened up the personal creation of the world by God to me more clearly, and especially God's presence in it. I didn't interpret this illumination as a form of pantheism but rather as a sign of God's immanence to us.

⁎⁎

Last evening, taking Charlie, my son, to his piano lesson at Loyola Marymount with Linda Love, I found the chapel open unexpectedly, all dark, with my favorite little place under the Blessed Sacrament tabernacle free. The Lord sent quiet and then a sense of his longing to have me with him every day so that he could love me and fill me with his Spirit. I wrote this poem:

En Route To Eternity

*O Lord, I love You
with a middle-aged
woman's heart
sick to death of
flattering fluttering loves
of my own making
cherishing innocence as a
nearly-extinct species.*

*Your love
too full to be feigned,
swoops down,
too heavy with mercy
for my body to sustain*

*Pinned like a dead butterfly
to the felt cardboard
of my despair*

*I try to fly
to Your heavenly hymn.*

*A jerky pas-de-deux at best
garbed in veils of tears.*

*At last Your Yes wins over
all my no's.*

*I blush
Yes, Lord, ever young
fill in all the spaces
in the program of my life
and waltz me to eternity.*

I was on the way to an anti-nuclear peace conference. On the way the Lord seemed to come to me very strongly. I asked Him if he really wanted me to go to such conferences. The answer I heard was this: "Lend these things your support, but your heart belongs to me."

Appendix

Since entering into deeper prayer, I have more doubts than before. I realize that it is easier for me to believe in the God of the philosophers, the God who is beautifully omnipresent, than to believe in a God who loves me enough to single me out for special graces. That seems much more incredible.

My house is stilled now, literally and spiritually for it is Easter Week and Martin left for Israel, the girls are at work and Charlie at school, so I have a whole week with solitude for many hours of the day. The moment everyone was gone, a great rapture came over me, not because I do not love them all, but because I have a great need for solitude with the Lord right now. It seems he wants me alone to comfort me for all the years of suffering. Before, I didn't let him heal my heart because I was busy and troubled about many things, like Martha. Now I should just let go.

For years I hung on Your cross
at last so cozy
I made its wood
into a coffin for my dreams

Now, boldly You open it
not afraid
of the stench of old rage

Tenderly, You uncoil
the shroud with Your own hands
the wounds tear
living waters flow
I swim in Your immensity
stunned by Your love.

My daughter, my Bride
to see your beauty
look not in the mirror on the wall
Look in My eyes.

My spiritual director, Fr. Rockwell Shaules, S.J., noticing my fears about making mistakes asked me if I thought God was like a delicate phantom. I laughed. You cannot alienate God unless you consciously decide to do so. He suggested that just as in a dance the male takes the lead, so I must let God take the lead. I should not try to control Him even if He makes a long pause in the dance.

Do not look at me, God
I am too ugly.
Not repelled,
You beckon me,
stroke my ruffled fur
distract me with small beauties,
then take my hand and ask
"Do you want to tell Me about it?"

Wondering how God could enjoy watching me all day doing my silly things, He seemed to answer with a corresponding question: how, then, can you enjoy watching a cat move about the house? For philosophers that is a prime question: why should a perfect God create imperfect creatures? The answer I give to my students is to glimpse the mystery by pondering their own love for lower creatures.

I run my heart
over the ridged Braille of reality
until I see Your face, my God.

Please pray for my dear husband. God is sanctifying him — a la Job — not the way of joy and illumination. Each day he becomes more long-suffering under various physical and mental trials.

Appendix

My mother recovered splendidly from the operation (for colon cancer performed when she was in her seventies). Best of all she came out of the anesthetic with the thought that she needed to forgive and be forgiven. She saw that only extreme fear of death can bring one to confess one's deepest sins. It was wonderful to sit by her bedside talking about deep matters after years of arguments and polite chit-chat.

I read somewhere that when we pray we should join our hands around all those we love, both embracing and giving them to God.

A nice line on a tape:
*"you have a choice —
be a fool for Christ or just an ordinary idiot."*

Lying in bed toward dawn God put me into a semi-trance. I saw in my mind an inner vision of His unity. Then the unity became brightness and the brightness the middle of a circle in which I could feel the oneness of everyone I love, then again just One, One, One, for God and Brightness.

The mystic eats what the metaphysician writes recipes for.

Detachment

*if all is nothing
shall I not ask a littler share?*

I am torn between the idea that home-life simply cannot be perfect and must be a suffering, and the thought that if I was more loving I would feel it as a sort of paradise in the sense of love. It is when I fail to see that every suffering in the family can be taken as a penance and instead construct some ideal image of family life that I become wretched and frustrated. Perhaps it is a matter of phases until I arrive at that great point of holiness where I am willing to suffer and endure and pray and hope but not complain and try to take-over, etc. It is much better than it used to be, praise God.

Stigmata of Family Life

nailed to their needs
pinioned to their demands
inescapably wounded by their wounds
you and they are one
all on one tree

My daughter Carla, who had trembled with fear all her life that her father would die, got so much reassuring grace after Martin died that she wrote this beautiful tribute, also included at the funeral:

Eulogy to Love

Rarely, one meets an individual whose definition is so outside the dictionary, who is so unique, that one is magnetized to his presence by question marks ... drawn to the inevitable exclamation point at the end of the final sentence.

One cannot sum up such a man, only surround him with a warm blanket of words, seeking for the contours of greatness in the outline.

My father, Martin Chervin, a man whose written words battered at every locked door, and rattled the chains of every skeleton in the celestial closet ... was largely a shy and intensely private man. I could speak volumes about what his life meant to me and to those he loved and yet we were never able to get from him more than the barest outline of the facts of his life, gleaned from a few hesitant sentences sprinkled from a clogged shaker. In the end, it is music that sums him up, the music he loved that is now his voice, the music that speaks another language, wordless, into the desolate night he left behind in my soul.

Appendix

Truly, he was most himself when anyone was in need: physical, emotional, or intellectual. He would swell from the confines of his chair and give and give and give until the very largeness of his giving would form an answer in the clouds, writ by a Father's hand: I AM LOVE.

I believe that it was the suicide of this immense love in the form of my brother's death that ultimately took him away, perhaps a few precious years before his time. But this is the death he chose for himself, in the manner he selected, his last song a cry from the heart toward his son ... whom we must imagine waiting eagerly in the wings with outstretched arms, answering the call with a heavenly composition all their own.

I counted and stored every moment with my father as currency of the heart, miserly with it and greedy ... I will forever have a triumph of riches in my life ... the ability to value the gifts of the heart and mind and soul. the awe to stand small at the majestic trumpet in a single chord from a master's strings ...

Now, I will reach into the darkness for the light within, knowing that somewhere there a friend is waiting, big and warm and safe and strong, even in the shadows, even in the twilight, even in the night ... I WILL NOT BE ALONE.

Carla Chervin Conley

✦✦✦✦✦✦✦✦✦✦ ✦ ✦✦✦✦✦✦✦✦✦✦ ✦ ✦✦✦✦✦✦✦✦✦✦ ✦ ✦✦✦✦✦✦✦✦✦✦ ✦ ✦✦✦✦✦✦✦✦✦✦ ✦

Diana wrote this a few months before Martin died and read it at the funeral.

Avrium (Martin's original name in Hebrew)
sits by his Momma's grave in silence,
thinking of the ones he loves, the ones he can't forget —
lives he touched with promise and regret
... he grabs the dirt and lets it trickle through his fingers,
now an old man — could it be? He?!!

The baker's son, he smells the fresh-baked loaves,
he sees his father's eyes, tired, late at night,
 a strong hand thoughtlessly patting his oldest son's curls:

En Route To Eternity

"My son, the one who will grow up to see great wonders happen..."
A father lost to sweat and toil, New York, the East Side,
not much time to hold a little boy ...
so love is spent in little coins under the pillow on Christmas Eve —
A Sabbath night, the candles lit,
he sees his father's hand raised in the air, the Sabbath prayer,
the rhythm fills that hot, hot, night,
the faces gathered round the table, flickering in the candle light —
Is there some meaning greater than a little boy can grasp?
A little boy who feels his soul soar high
above the tenement rooftops
Up to the stars
'til Momma's pinch brings him down to earth again.

And Avrium would change his name and go to sea,
leaving the rich warm scent of bread behind,
he grabs at life with both hands
clutching at the railing,
and feels the sweet, sweet breezes whistle by ...
But what does it all mean?
His restless mind worries truth like a dog with a bone,
and then buries the questions in favor of some new adventure.
Momma worries for him,
shows his postcards to the neighborhood: "My son! The explorer!" –
passed among the sour pickles, stained with unshed tears ...
And life so sweet it melts on the tongue
for the young who think they have all the answers —
Martin Chervin, newly named,
holds fragile life with both hands tight,
so little sand now trickles through the fingers
loose upon the railing,
Momma's pinch is just a lingering echo on the telephone ...

A man can master everything except his father's death,
and even then go on to claim his soul ...
A man can read in books and find a beauty
that can cut his heart in two
and make him hold his breath.
A man can try to write of this,
and cast his words away, not once, a thousand times —
and still — one finger poking at the keys — can try again.

Appendix

A man can hear his life in music, birth to death,
breathing his last day with the last note ...
A man can wake with tears falling down his face,
wake in the night with longing for his lost home ...
And if he go back home again,
a man can reach back
groping through lost time for a little boy he used to be,
and losing the hand he hoped to grasp,
a man can look his mother in the face with hate and love ...
a man can look his brother in the face with hate and love...

Ex-Avruim, there's wisdom gathered after pain.
And suddenly, a woman, young, naive.
And suddenly, a light that wasn't there before:
a reason for the pain,
the music reaches a crescendo —
the world curtsies shyly —
"Share your sandwich with me, please?"
And if you see the gap between my life and yours,
then bridge it with a ring that screams "FOREVER!"
and Gretchen to your Faust,
she saves your soul with bonds of need unspoken you can't sever.

There are little starlings born within his heart
that take shape on this earth as little girls.
To be Daddy now is sweeter than the world
he held between his fingers not so long before.

You've dipped your finger in the finest chocolate,
and wake up one day gasping for your breath — a nightmare scene,
The Scream by Munsch —
a cacophony of siren-light fades in and out,
a panic in your mind,
a panic rasping, heaving, grasping,
breathing briefly for what's left undone —
clutching at one word,
and then your mind goes black until you feel a pinch ...
"Momma?" you wonder,
but again you're screaming,
dreaming of the world you owned not long before —
and wouldn't it be easier to let it slip away, away, awayyy ... ?

En Route To Eternity

Avruim smiles grimly by his Mamma's grave —
he knows that pain was nothing to the pain to come —
and with a trembling finger draws a symbol on the earth —
a cross? an X?
Depends on your perspective.

A man can look at Jesus in the face,
and lightened by a tiny glimpse of heaven,
can choose, yet, still a longer walk on earth.
A man can search inside his soul and find some atom of will,
some hunger to go on — can grip his bed, can raise his head,
can look into the light —
can patiently await release,
can stand again on his two feet,
can stand up strong against the glare and choose...
Martin looking at his newborn son,
incubated, fighting for his life —
his blue eyes pierce the plastic
"You will live!"
and slowly, those unfocused eyes meet his —
a tiny hand lifts up as though to call a toast to life —
a well of love that forces life to be —
a moment when time freezes and stands still.

As a writer, there is ample time to love a tiny boy —
strong fingers through the curly hair,
"you are my son!
And you will live to change the world in wondrous ways ..."
 And he would grow to share his father's joy in life,
in music, in the written word —
if ever two were one, it was these two —
linked by a bond that's rarely seen or felt.

A man can see his son's strong light grow dim —
a man can give of all he is to save it —
a man can climb in darkness through the narrow paths,
screaming within his soul with all his might.
A man can give up sleep for many nights,
and face the day resolved to win the fight —
a man can hold his son's small face within both hands,
and breathe like the Creator on the clay,

Appendix

a man can hold his breath and whisper a last prayer,
and let go, praying he is doing right...

There is a horror in the letting go,
insanity lies grimacing round every corner —
and how can you say
"Rest in peace, my only son"
and not remember Isaac, innocent, before the slaughter.
There is true misery in going on —
impossible you say —
and yet I do;
surrounded by my dreams of him,
living for some sign from him,
weeping at night,
counting the days —
amazed and appalled that so much time is passed —
at last, a shadow world of nothing held between my hands —
reaching heavenward with nought but hope,
begging God
"Please, please, my boy, my life"
groping for patience,
groping for belief....

Avruim sitting by Momma's grave –
Oscuro passes gently from the sky,
and unbeknownst to him,
prostrate before the grave,
waiting for Momma's pinch
for Poppa's sigh,
a ray of light streaks grandly from the heavens,
an unseen hand sweeps softly through his curly hair,
an unheard voice whispers with pride
"You are my son!
And you will see great wonders, yet,
believe it, and hold the hands of both your son and mine....   "

Martin Chervin 1992

The Miriam Press publishes literature focusing on the People of Israel within the Catholic Church. This literature is intended to serve their needs and to address the issues related to their identity as Catholic Israelites.

The Miriam Press also serves as the publishing arm of the Association of Hebrew Catholics (AHC). The AHC publication, *The Hebrew Catholic,* is published six times per year.

Jewish Identity by Elias Friedman, OCD, the first book published by The Miriam Press, is a prophetic reading of the *signs of the times.* Fr. Friedman's magnum opus provides the historical and theological background of the AHC. Msgr. Eugene Kevane contributed the preface and Ronda Chervin, PH.D. wrote the introduction.

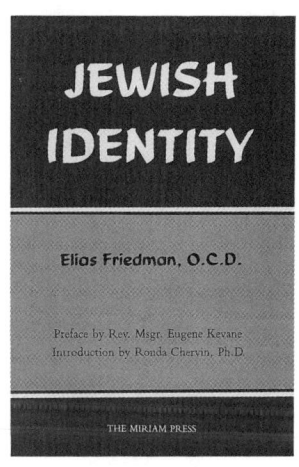

The Association of Hebrew Catholics is a lay apostolate *in* and *for* the Church. It aims at ending the alienation of Catholics of Jewish origin from their historical identity and background, by the formation of a Hebrew Catholic Community juridically approved by the Holy See.

The *kerygma* of the AHC announces that the divine plan of salvation has entered the phase of the *Apostasy of the Gentiles,* prophesied by Our Lord and St. Paul, and of which the *Return of the Jews to the Holy Land* is a corollary.

The Miriam Press booklist or a sample copy of *The Hebrew Catholic* may be obtained by writing to:

PO Box 798, Highland NY 12528 U.S.A.